Money & ME University®

In God We Trust

PowerPoint Guide

Words of Wisdom - WOW Edition

Sara Money

About the Author

Sara Money is an expert in providing a financial literacy education system for organizations who are inspired to help people who are living in survival mode (i.e. paycheck to paycheck).

- Author of eleven books on financial literacy
- MA in Counseling, 1998, *Webster University*
- BA in Psychology and Communication, 1992, *University of New Mexico (UNM)*
- Counselor, APS (*Albuquerque Public Schools)*
- City Coordinator for DVULI *(DeVos Urban Leadership Initiative)*
- Executive Director, *Love INC (In the Name of Christ) of Albuquerque*
- Clearinghouse Director*, Love INC (In the Name of Christ) of Albuquerque*
- Counselor and Residential Advisor, Job Corps
- Income Support Specialist, *New Mexico Human Services Department*
- Volunteer, *Rape Crisis Center, Shelter for Victims of Domestic Violence*, *UNM Agora Crisis Center*

And...in case you were wondering, Sara Money is her real name. She was born with it!

ISBN 10: 0-9966189-6-1
ISBN 13: 978-0-9966189-6-0

Money & ME: PowerPoint Guide

Letter from Sara

Who can survive on $1,000 a month? The reality is many people throughout the United States who are living on disability or earning minimum wage live on this amount. It is a struggle for people to pay for housing, food, and clothing as the cost of living increases in America. This increase is dramatically affecting the lives of low-income individuals and families. In July 2011, I was challenged to teach classes to low-income people on how to better manage their money.

My first attempt was to use money management concepts from proven financial literacy programs for middle-income people. I quickly discovered that low-income people were not familiar with terms like "vacations," "dry cleaning," and "life insurance;" using those words was like speaking another language. People with low incomes were familiar with acronyms like "TANF," "SNAP," and "SSI," which may seem foreign to middle-income people. In addition to finding a new language, I discovered a new culture. It was interesting and exciting to learn cultural differences and discover a different world within my own community.

The *Money & ME Program* is designed to be simple, easy to understand, and help people learn how to take control of their money. If low-income people can learn and apply one of these concepts, they can begin the process of gaining control of managing their money. We have seen people save $300 per month when they stop buying chips, soda, and renting movies daily from convenience stores. People who have implemented the concepts we teach have been able to pay off money owed and have learned to live within their income levels. I realized that many people, such as those living on Social Security or disability, may always be considered low-income; none the less, I have seen the excitement when they realize they can have financial freedom.

Money & ME began with a basic budget worksheet adjusted to the language that low-income people speak. Now it is a complete workbook with PowerPoint Guide and training. Many people helped in the development, including conducting extensive research and participating in focus groups. All the concepts and ideas taught are meant to be simple but life changing.

Money & ME facilitators need to understand the language and culture of low-income people in order to effectively help them. Volunteers from various professions have attended "Train the Trainer Team" classes to learn how to teach and coach these participants.

I invite you to become part of the *Money & ME Program*. You may become a Trainer, a Coach, or a participant. The important thing to remember is for *Money & ME* to be successful people must be willing to change their own habits and ways of thinking. You were created by God and He has a special purpose for you. I pray that you will walk with Him through this process to start a journey of making better choices that will impact your life for years to come.

Sara Money, Creator and Owner of Money & ME

Acknowledgements

From day one, this program has been a collaboration of many people, which included extensive research and focus groups. Each time the *Money & ME Program* was taught, things were added and improvements were made. Each person regardless of his / her role gave insight into the development of *Money & ME*. This program would not have happened without God's inspiration and the amazing people He brought together.

It is a pleasure and honor to thank the following people:

My family:

- My daughter, Cassie, who helped with childcare, editing, development, and teaching.
- My daughter, Emily, who inspired me to keep the *Money & ME Program* simple.
- My mom, Charlene Greenwood, for proofing worksheets, PowerPoint presentations, and curriculum, often late at night to help meet program deadlines.

Editors:

- Lauren Leggee, Love INC's Administrative Assistant, sharing insight into the low-income world, helping develop focus groups, and sometimes being "the focus group."
- Tori Pilcher, Love INC's Donation Center Manager and *Money & ME* Coordinator / Trainer, "pulling together" the many components, advising on redesign of worksheets, and revising content.
- Matthew Valerio-Hirschfeld, Ph.D., professor and advisor at Trinity Southwest University, assisted with scripture references and development.
- Glenda Austin, Administrator, Registrar at Trinity Southwest University, for her insight and assistance with graphic design.
- Paula Avery, Mike Henderson, and Yvonne Lara, Love INC's Writing Club, for feedback.

Others:

- Edith Carreon, Love INC's Clearinghouse / Helpline Manager, for translating everything into Spanish and sharing insight into the Hispanic culture.
- Love INC's 2014 Board of Directors for their prayers and support.
- Mickey Beisman, attorney, who gave legal advice and encouragement.
- Mike Cosgrove, Executive Director of True North Financial Ministries, for sharing his knowledge and expertise of money management principles.

Table of Contents

Trainer Stories to be Prepared Ahead of Time

The purpose of Trainer Stories is to allow the Trainers opportunities to share personal stories, add personal interest, and help build relationships. Trainers should prepare their stories ahead of time.

REMEMBER: Trainer stories need to be BRIEF! A graphic with the wording "My Story" is on the slide to remind you when to share your story.

Trainer Story #1: Think of a story about something you did as a child that cost your parent(s) money, or an unexpected expense you incurred related to your own children. *Session 1: Reality Check*

____

____

____

Trainer Story #2: Think of something you used to purchase, but when you realized how much it was costing you a year, you stopped making that purchase. *Session 1: Reality Check*

____

____

____

Trainer Story #3: Think of a time you experienced a burden (crisis) in your life. Maybe it was a family, medical, natural disaster, etc. Did you have other people around to help you? Talk about how having a support system in place can help especially when experiencing something unexpected. *Section 2: Responsibility*

____

____

____

Trainer Story #4: Share a story about how your parents handled money or how they taught you to handle money. *Session 2: Responsibility*

Trainer Story #5: Think of an unhealthy habit you once had. When did you realize it was unhealthy and how did you change it? *Session 2: Responsibility*

Trainer Story #6: Share a story about what you did as a kid to earn extra money. *Session 3: Smart Shopping*

Trainer Story #7: Share a brief story about whether you are a spender or a saver. What lessons have you learned? *Session 5: Build a Budget*

Trainer Story #8: Share a story about an activity you like to do that is free or costs very little money. NOTE: If your class is running out of time, you can leave out the "Free Activities" discussion and assign it as a homework project. *Session 6: Take Control*

Important Information

PowerPoint Design

There are six PowerPoint presentations. Each one is approximately one hour long. Each slide has animations and is designed for the Trainer to click one time to advance to the next slide. The words and animations are timed for casual speech for flow with the presentation. You can advance to the next session during the last discussion of each session if doing more than one in a day.

Trainers SHOULD practice all presentations to become familiar with the content, animations, and flow! Prepare Trainer stories ahead of time. Make sure the stories are appropriate for the audience.

Distribution of Workbooks & Kits

It is important for participants to NOT take home their workbooks and kits until the last session if you are doing the program over a period of time. They will most likely not remember to bring them back and it is important they have the materials for all the sessions. If you are doing the program in a one-day format, then they will be able to take home their workbooks and kits at the end.

Meals

If the program will be done in one day, plan on providing a simple but nutritious meal for participants i.e. soups, sandwiches, Frito pie, casseroles, etc. if doing as an all-day program. It is helpful to have other people come in to help with this part of the program. Setting up the food, serving, and clean-up should NOT be done by the Assistant Trainer or the Trainer. That will take away from their jobs. Participants enjoy the meal and being served. It is great relationship building time.

Session 1: Reality Check

Slide 1

Slide 2

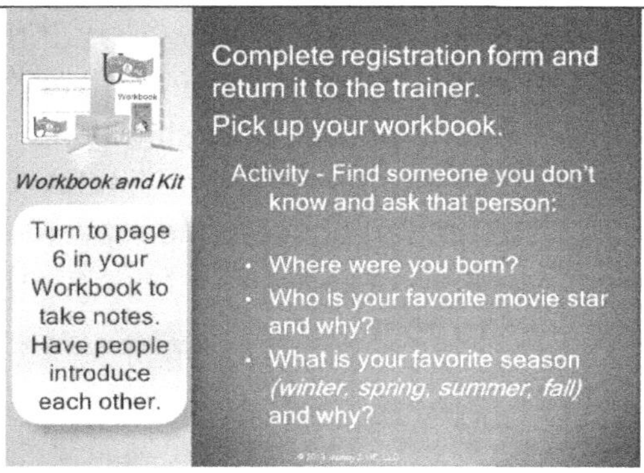

This slide should be on display while participants are coming in. The Trainer and other helpers should use it as a guide to instruct participants on what they should be doing during check-in. The questions are to help participants meet and greet others. *Money & ME* focuses on building healthy relationships. This activity helps to get the process started. Have each person introduce the person he or she just met.

Slide 3

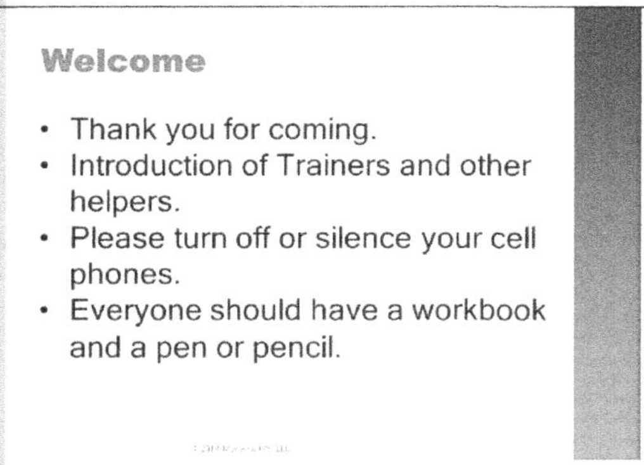

As the Trainer, make sure you know where the restrooms, childcare, and emergency exits are located. Hold up your cell phone, use it as a visual reminder for people to turn off (or put on vibrate) their cell phones. Make sure everyone has a *Money & ME Workbook* and a pencil. The Lead Trainer needs to "engage" with the audience; he or she should be energetic and excited to teach the class!

Slide 4

Show each item (receipt organizer, note pad, envelopes, and a pencil) to reinforce the slide.
Each person 16 years or older will receive a workbook and kit. The participant will get the kit during the workshop.

Slide 5

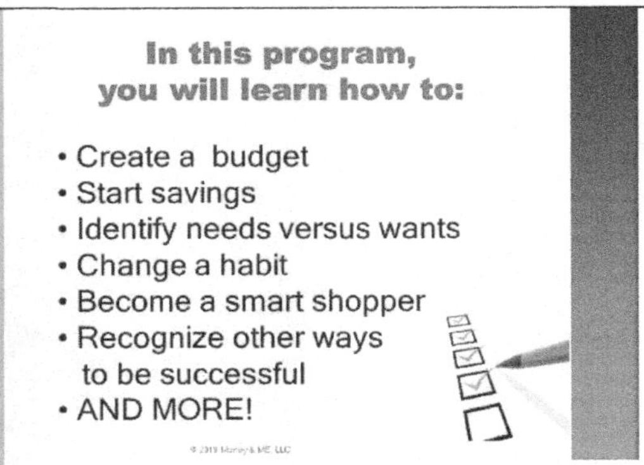

Most PowerPoint slides are set for one click with the clicker.

Slide 6

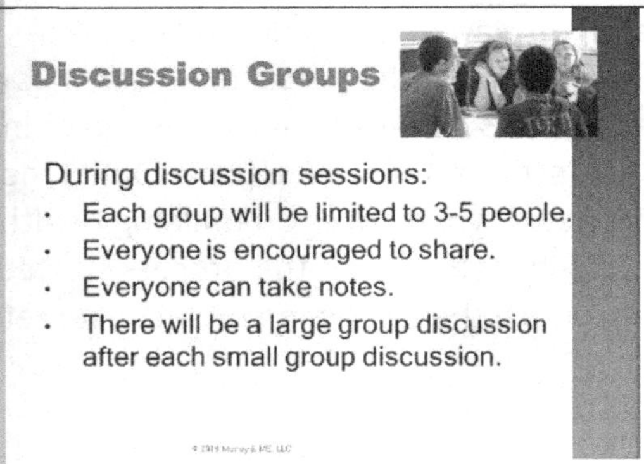

The Trainer and Assistant Trainer should NOT be part of the small group discussions. Trainers should walk around and encourage discussion, but let the participants share and learn from one another. Small groups should be limited to 3 – 5 people. If the groups are too large, everyone may not get a chance to participate. Remind groups to stay on topic. Most discussion times are 5 to 15 minutes.

Slide 7

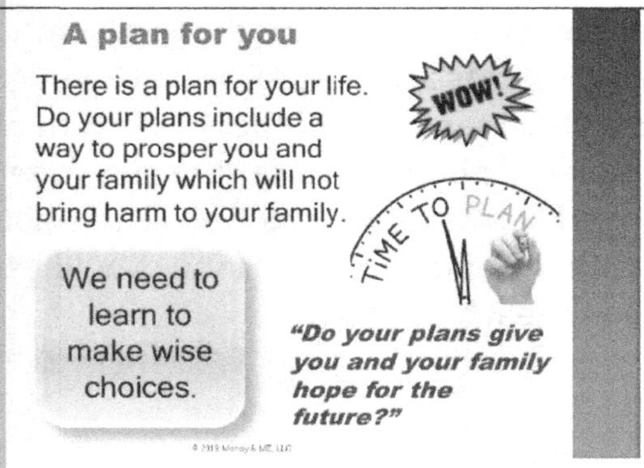

It is very important for participants to have a plan for their life and make wise choices.

Slide 8

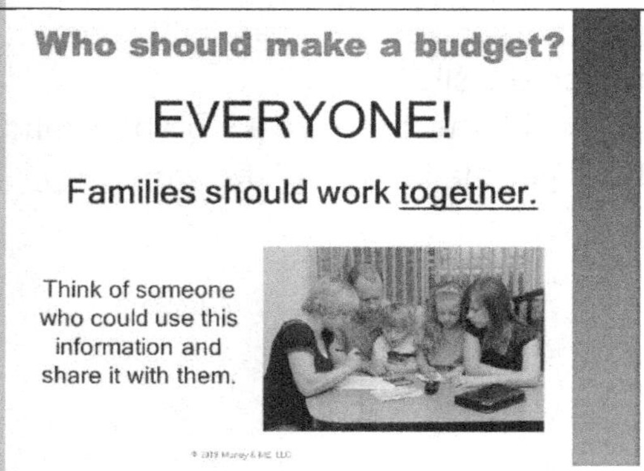

Families are encouraged to work together when creating their budget. Encourage participants to share the information they are going to learn with others. The highest level of learning happens when a person is able to share their knowledge with others.

Slide 9

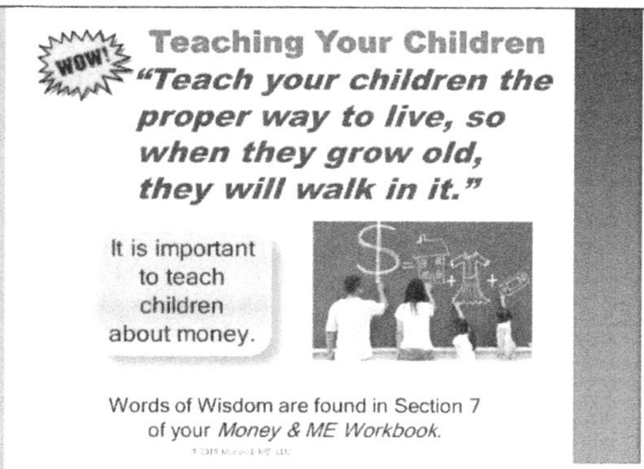

In Section 7 of the *Money & ME Workbook* is a list of all Words of Wisdom used in the *Money & ME Program*.

Slide 10

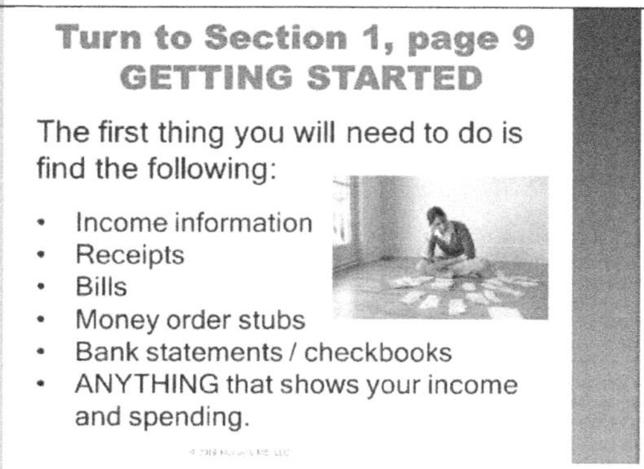

This will be some of their homework.
Remind them, this information is private and is not to be shared with the group.

Slide 11

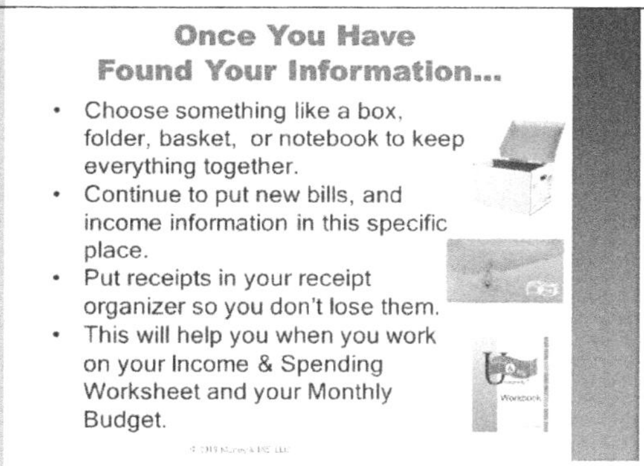

Encourage the participants to find something they can use to keep their financial information together. The more organized people become, the better they will be with paying their bills on time.

Slide 12

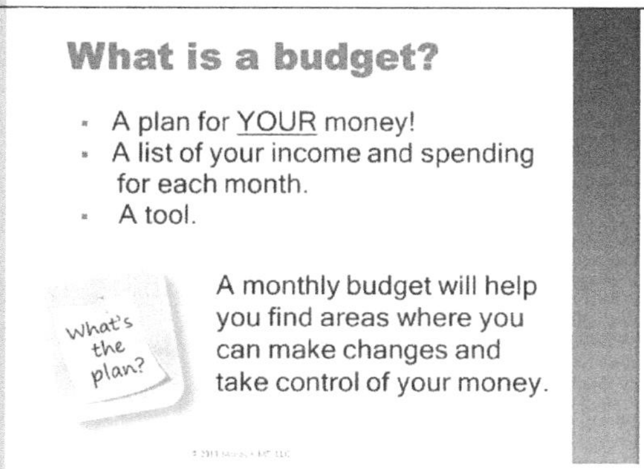

"Budget" might be a NEW or SCARY word for some participants. Remind them, a budget is a **"plan"** to help them with their money needs and goals. Following a budget occurs over time. Keys to their success are: being patient with one another, working together, and adjusting their budget as needed.

Slide 13

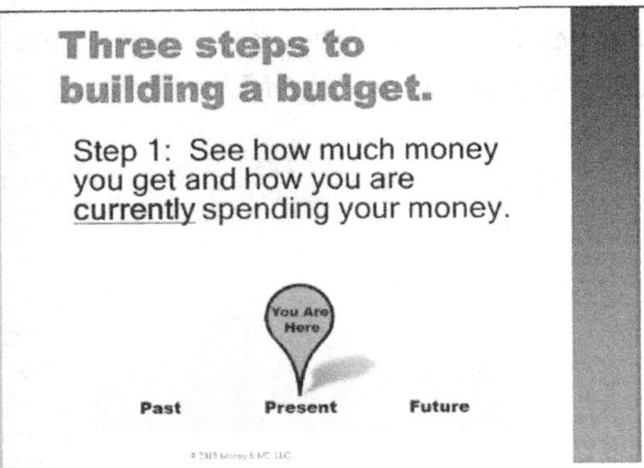

Building a budget is a process. The first step is identifying how much income a person (or household has) and how much he or she is currently spending. This will be done by completing the Monthly Income & Spending Worksheet.

Slide 14

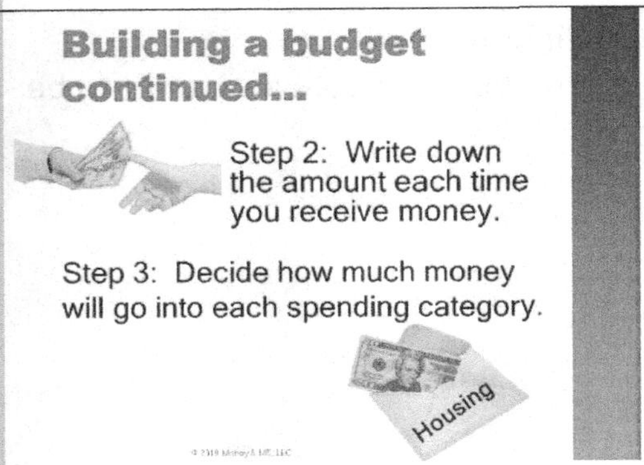

The second step is to write down each time a person receives a paycheck.

The third step is writing down how much money you want to spend in each category.

Slide 15

This analogy is to help participants see that it is important to know their current spending habits. They need to know what they are currently doing (YOU ARE HERE) before they can get to where they want to go (THEIR FUTURE BUDGET AND SPENDING HABITS).

Slide 16

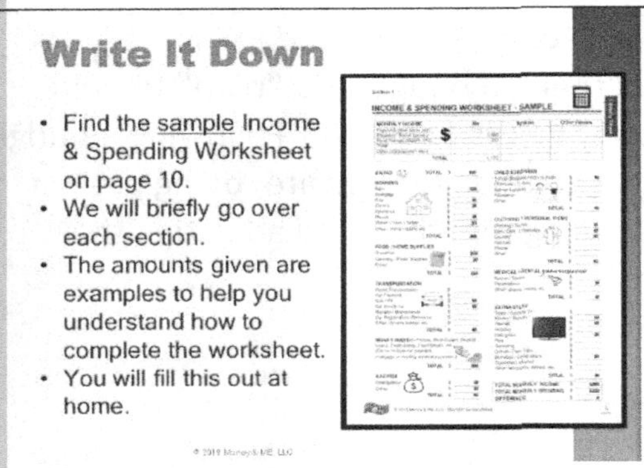

Income & Spending Worksheet

The Income & Spending Worksheet lays the FOUNDATION for the rest of the *Money & ME Program*. This may be the first time participants have written their income and spending on paper. Each workbook includes two copies of the Income & Spending Worksheet. One copy will be used during orientation. The extra two are so they can use them for future use.

Slide 17

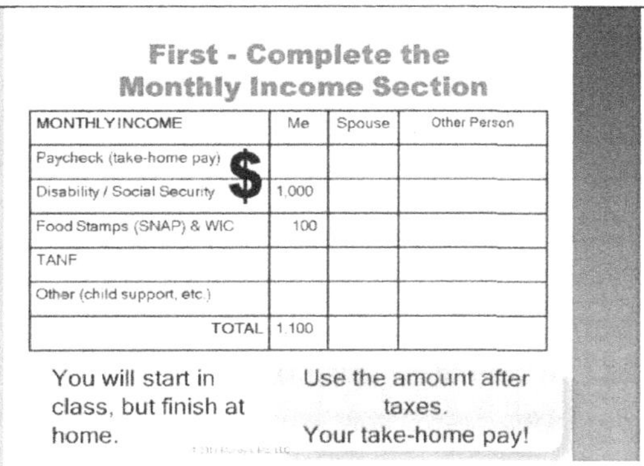

Participants need to know how much money they have to work with each month. Food stamps (SNAP), WIC and TANF are all considered income.
Their monthly income and monthly budget are figured on their income after taxes have been withheld.
REMEMBER: This is to be an overview.

Slide 18

Spending categories are the foundation of the Cash Envelope System. We will discuss this more during the workshop. The concept of spending categories may be NEW to most people.
Trainers can point to different pictures and emphasize some of the categories.

Slide 19

Every participant is different. Some may be giving to the community and some may not. That is OK. We want them to begin thinking of ways to give. Our community becomes stronger when we give back. It is also important to get participants to always think about what they are getting (an entitlement perspective) to what they could be giving.

Slide 20

Giving back to our community and helping others are important. Share a few ways people can give back such as cleaning the neighborhood, picking up trash at a school, washing a car, cleaning a yard, volunteering, etc.

Slide 21

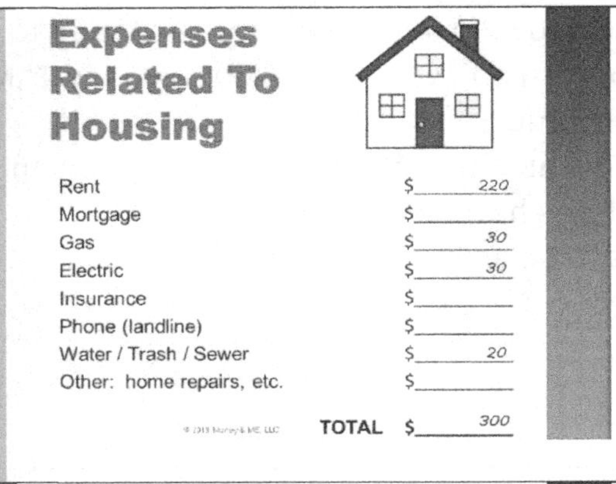

Acknowledge HOUSING can be a difficult area to make changes. However, if a person or family is spending more than 30% of their monthly income on housing it will greatly reduce other spending categories. Options to consider for reducing housing expenses may include moving to a different place, applying for subsidized housing, budget billing, etc. Home phone (landline) should be listed in this category. Cell phones can be listed here or in the clothing and personal items section.

Slide 22

Some people may be living in a group home, be homeless, or still living with their parents. Even if they are not paying for housing right now, it is very important for them to start putting money into this category. They will need to have money for a damage deposit and at least the first month's rent.

Slide 23

During the workshop, we will talk about ways to save money in this area. The amount of money spent on food and cleaning supplies may surprise them.

Slide 24

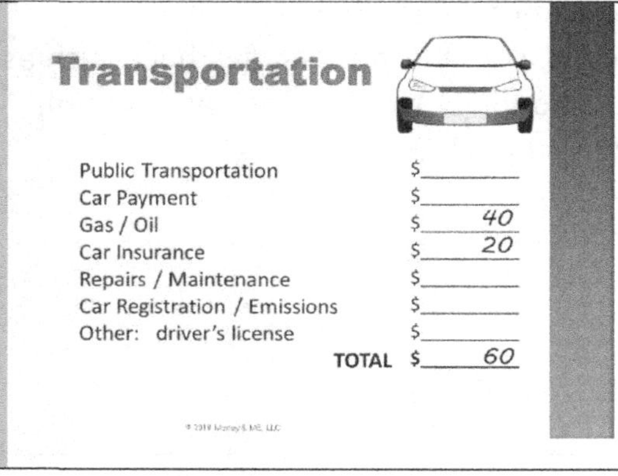

This is another area where participants might be able to make changes.
During the workshop we will discuss a few transportation money-saving tips.

Slide 25

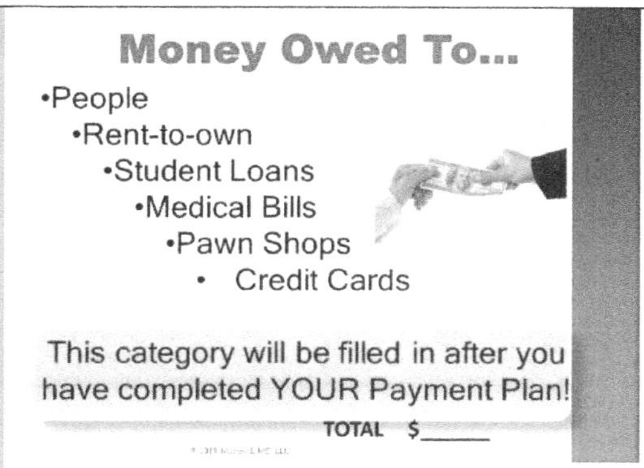

Participants may owe money for different things such as: payday loans, title loans, pawn shops, family members, landlords, credit cards, etc.
This section will be completed AFTER participants have completed a Payment Plan!

Slide 26

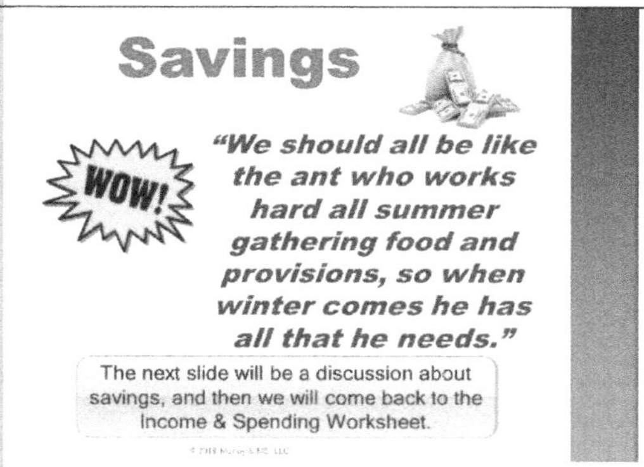

Savings

SAVINGS may also be a new idea for some participants. This can also be a sensitive topic.

Slide 27

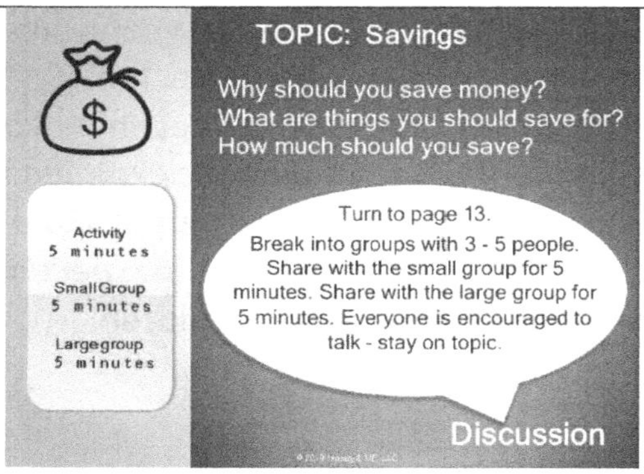

DISCUSSIONS ARE THE MOST IMPORTANT PART OF WORKSHOPS! Participants are relating to each other and learning for themselves.
This is the first group discussion and should not be skipped. This discussion is on savings and you (the Trainer) will find it interesting to learn what is important to them. Every group will be different and you (the Trainer) will learn a lot. Encourage the participants to share. The Trainer should be listening!

Slide 28

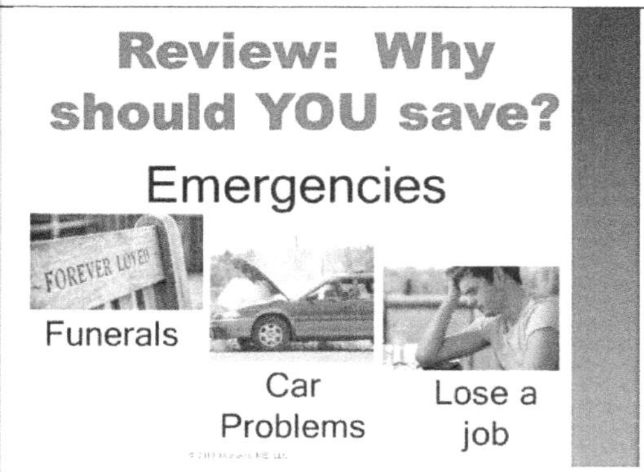

Hopefully during the discussion time, the participants identified different emergencies that they should be saving for.

Slide 29

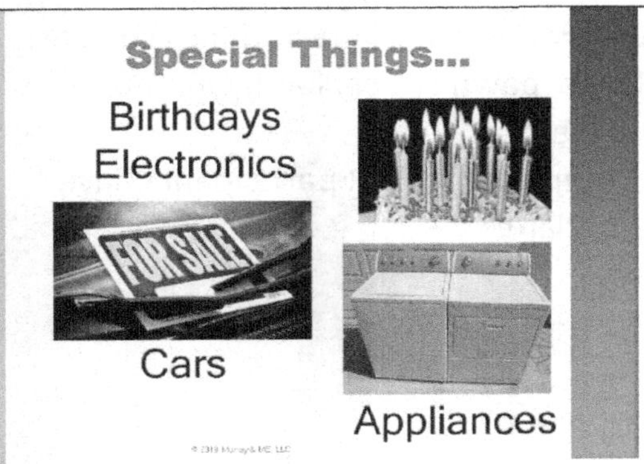

Everyone likes to purchase special things. It is important for participants to save for things they want instead of borrowing money. Review the different things that people may save money for.

Slide 30

Participants can choose what is important to them and begin saving for specific purchases.

Slide 31

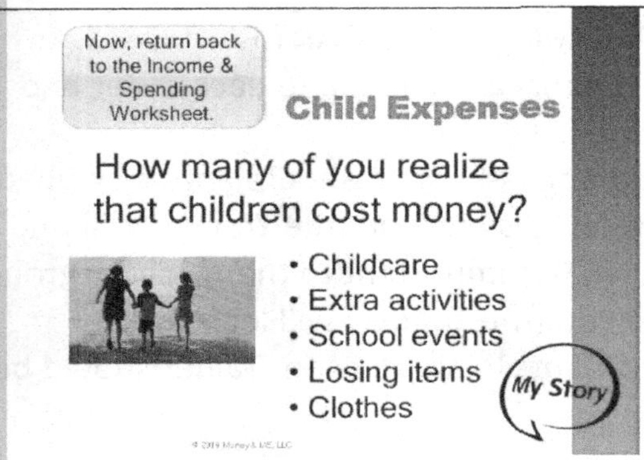

Prepare ahead of time a <u>personal story</u> about when you were surprised by an unexpected child expense. It might be a child losing a VERY expensive textbook. Stories should be <u>funny and encouraging</u>, NOT about a traumatic experience. **Trainer Story**: **Think of a story about something you did as a child that cost your parent(s) money, or an unexpected expense you incurred related to your own children.**

Slide 32

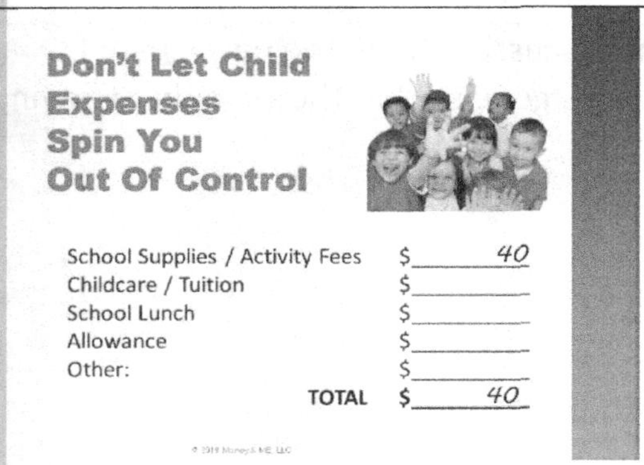

This is another area where participants may be able to make changes
REMEMBER: This is to be an overview.

Slide 33

Have fun with this slide! It is good to get the participants agreeing that clothes are important. No one showed up naked.

Slide 34

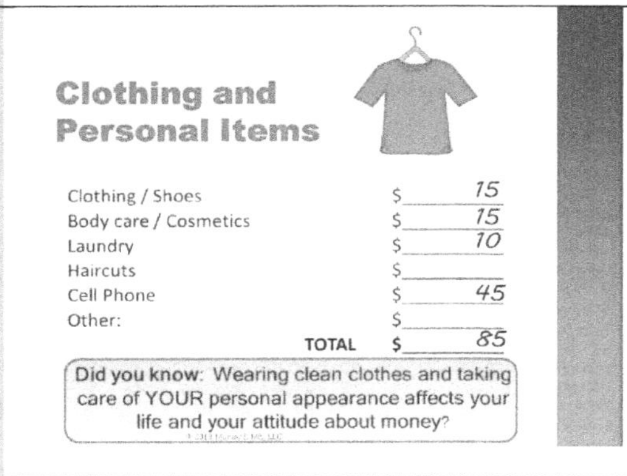

Wearing clean clothes and taking care of their personal appearance can affect their attitude about money. Cell phones can also be listed in this area. If they are paying for a phone for their children, is this something that the child can be earning himself or herself?

Slide 35

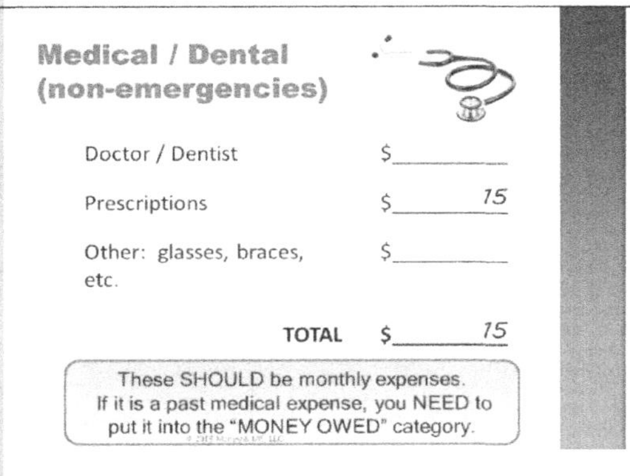

Some participants will have Medicaid and do not have to pay for this area. Others will have no health care insurance at all and may owe a lot of medical expenses. You do not need to spend a lot of time in this area, just acknowledge this as a spending category.

Slide 36

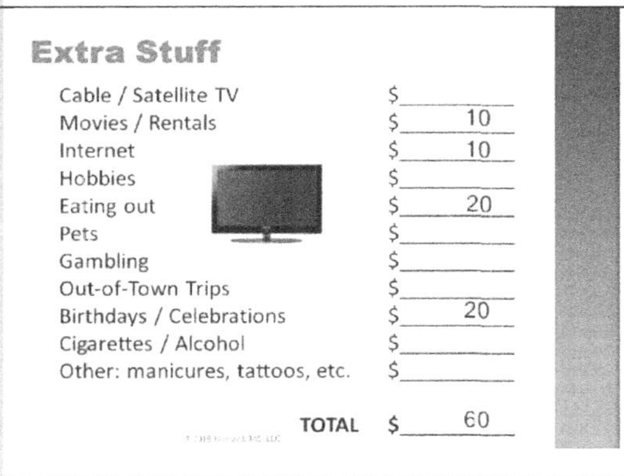

The last expense category on the Income & Spending Worksheet is an area where MANY changes can be made. Most people don't realize how much they are spending on extra stuff because they don't write it down. This is a category you will spend extra time discussing during the workshop.

REMEMBER: This is to be an overview.

Slide 37

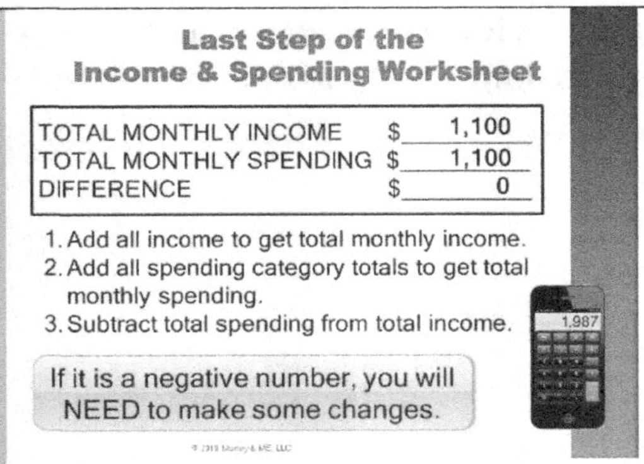

When participants complete this part of the Income & Spending Worksheet they will realize if they are living within their means or overspending.

Slide 38

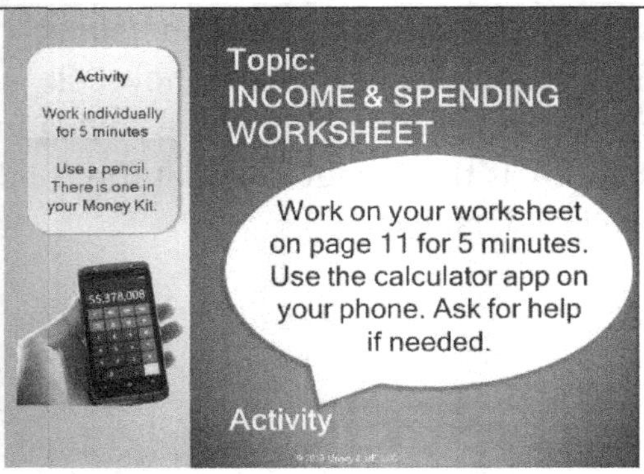

Have participants take a few minutes to work on their Income & Spending Worksheet. Remind them to use the pencil that is in their Money Kit.
Now have them use a calculator to figure out the annual expense. Walk around the room and assist with this process. Ask the group to share.

Slide 39

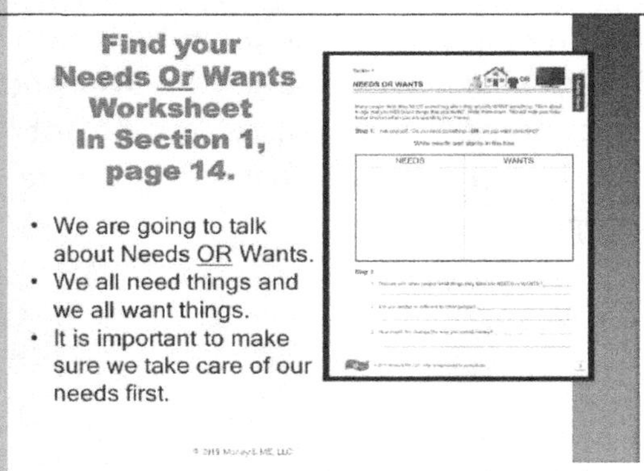

Discussion of Needs OR Wants can be interesting. People identify Needs OR Wants very differently.
Do not tell them what is a need or what is a want. Give participants the freedom to have an open discussion in this area.

Slide 40

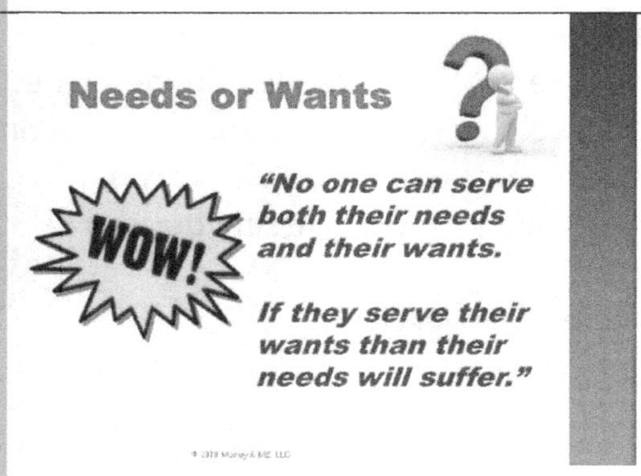

Needs or Wants. It is impossible for people to devote their time, money, and energy to two masters. Participants need to recognize what their wants are and what their needs are.

Slide 41

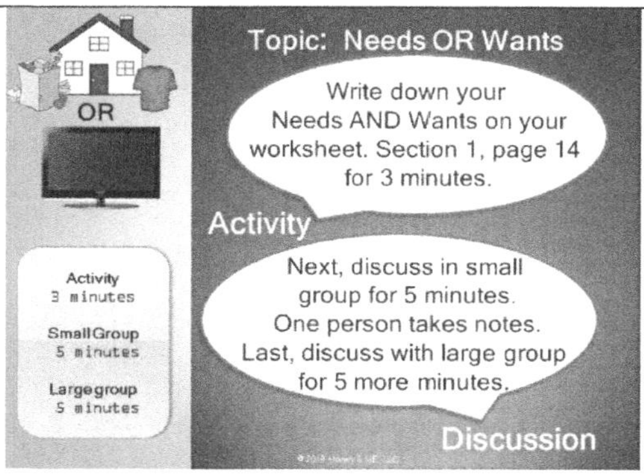

Once again, DO NOT skip the discussion activities. This is where the REAL learning takes place. Encourage participants to share what they have learned.

Slide 42

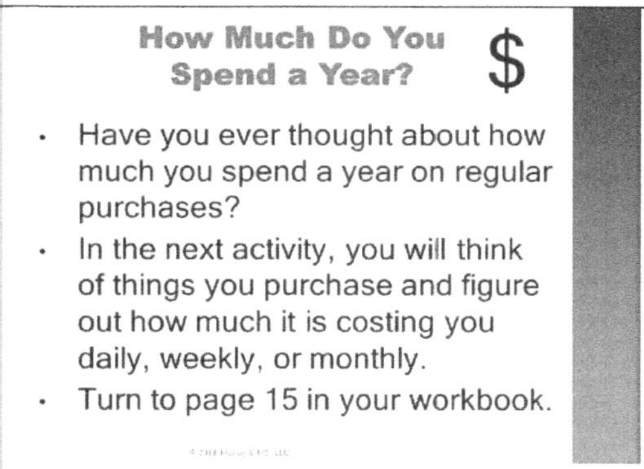

How Much Do You Spend A Year?

It is very important for participants to see how much they are spending a year on regular purchases.

Slide 43

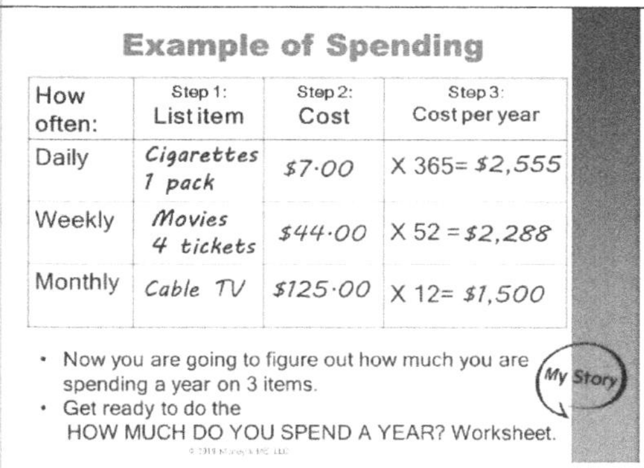

Go through the formula of how to figure out the annual expense.

Trainer Story: Share a story of something you used to purchase on a regular basis. When you realized how much it was costing you per year, did you stop buying the item? Were you surprised when you did this activity?

Slide 44

Have participants take a few minutes to think of items they purchase on a regular basis.

Now have them use a calculator to figure out the annual expense. Walk around the room and assist with this process. Ask the group to share.

Session 2: Responsibility

Slide 1

Reminder to open in prayer if doing this session on a different day.

Slide 2

Things to Do! Participants need to identify what are their responsibilities and what responsibilities belong to other people. Being able to take care of their own responsibilities will help them to stay in control of their lives. It is important for participants to not be enablers for people who are not taking care of their responsibilities.

Slide 3

It is important for participants to identify their daily, weekly, and monthly responsibilities. When people do not take care of their regular responsibilities, they can create a very difficult situation. It is important for them to not only identify their responsibilities but also take care of their own responsibilities.

Slide 4

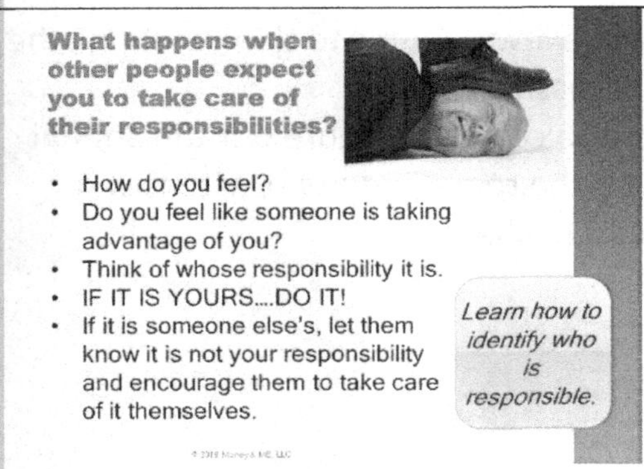

It is important for people to identify if others are trying to use or take advantage of them. By identifying who is responsible for things, it will help people discern if they need to help. This helps establish healthy boundaries.

Slide 5

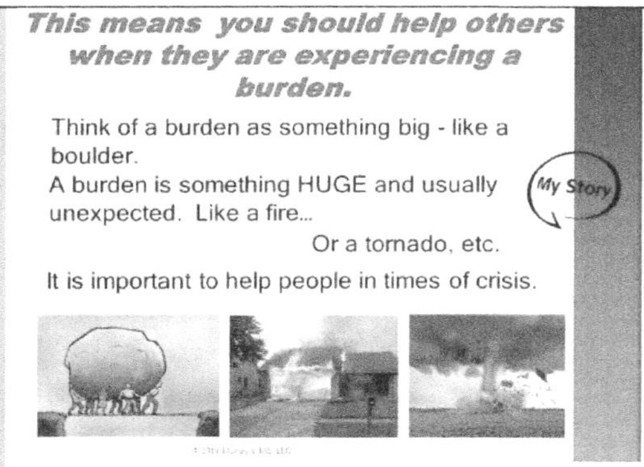

It is important to identify when it is appropriate to help others and when they should take care of things themselves. People should help others when it is something outside of their control. However, they should not help people take care of their responsibilities. That would be enabling and does not help others.

TRAINER STORY: Think of a time you were experiencing a burden (crisis). Maybe it was family, medical, natural disaster, etc. Talk about if you had a support system in place to help you or if you had to deal with it by yourself. Emphasis that it is good to have healthy relationships to help in times of crisis.

Slide 6

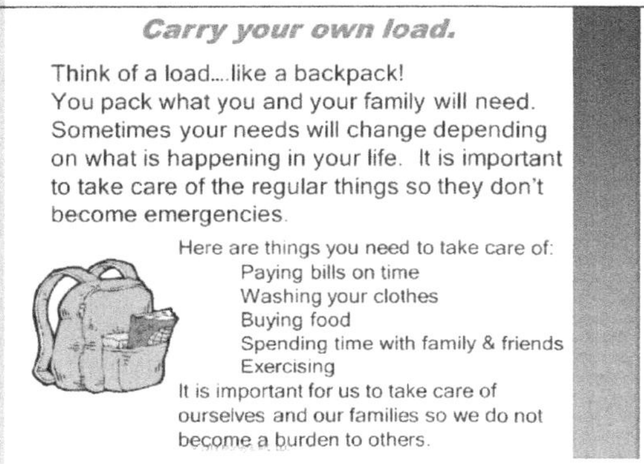

Many participants need to learn the importance of taking care of their daily, weekly, and monthly responsibilities. It is not good for them to expect others to do things for them. These basic concepts can help participants make changes that could have a long-lasting impact on their lives.

Slide 7

An important part in being able to help others when they need help OR receiving help in an emergency is by developing healthy relationships. The *Money & ME Program* focuses on relationship building by the discussions and activities throughout the curriculum.

Slide 8

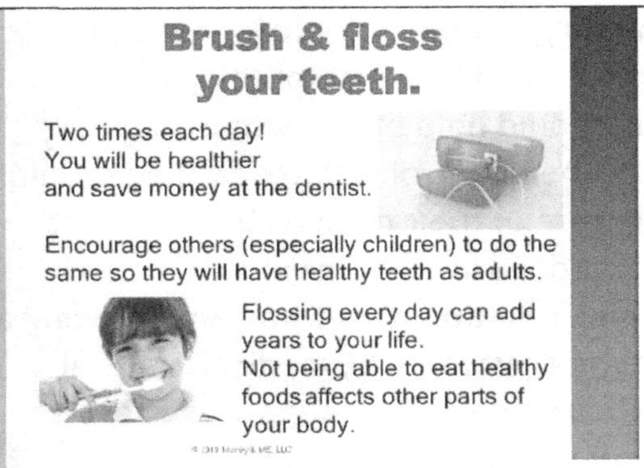

Good dental care can save them money in the long run, especially for children. People who have bad teeth have a harder time getting jobs than people who have good teeth.

Slide 9

It is important for participants to learn basic car maintenance if they have cars. If they don't take care of little things cars can become major expenses later. Ask participants how much it would cost if they ran their car out of oil. (A LOT!). Then ask how much it cost to check the oil and do regular oil changes.

Slide 10

When laundry is out of control, people may feel like their lives are out of control. Helping people get in control of their laundry will help them be more successful in life.

Slide 11

Some people don't realize there are 5 steps to getting laundry done. Helping to break the process into 5 steps can help people take control of their laundry.

Slide 12

Sometimes people will not have the time or money to go to a laundromat. They can wash their clothes at home.

Slide 13

This website is a great resource for people who need help getting organized in their homes.

Slide 14

Funerals are extremely expensive. Low-income people usually don't have money saved for their own funeral costs. Encourage them to get "Term Life Insurance" for the unexpected.

Slide 15

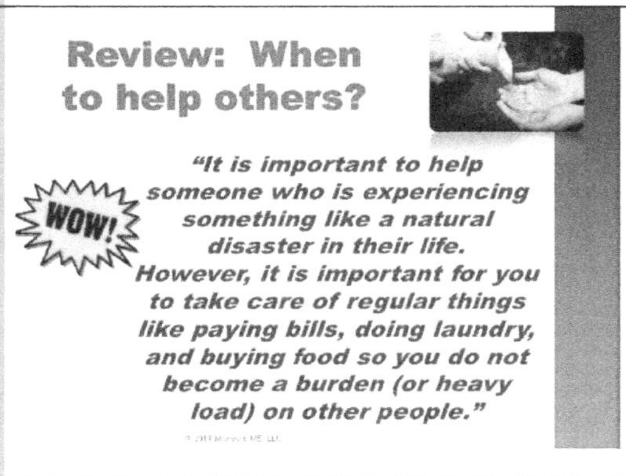

Helping others versus ourselves

So many times, we see low-income people give others money when they don't have enough money to pay their own bills. Someone may be "stalking" them to find out when they get money. Then the "stalker" tells a sad story to get money from that person. Use this slide and the next three slides to guide them as to when God says it is OK to help people and when they should take care of themselves.

Slide 16

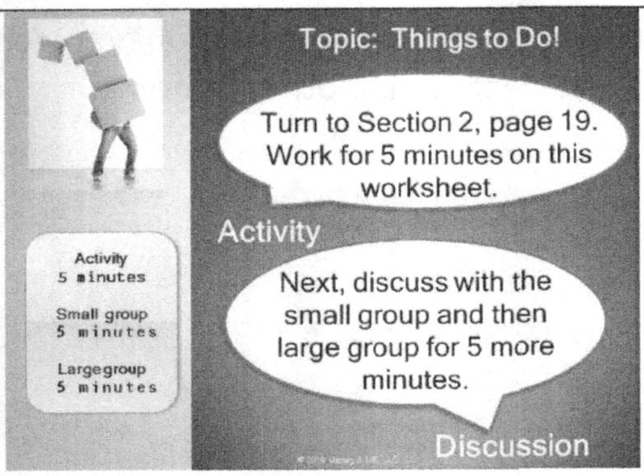

Encourage participants to think about their own loads. What can they do to make sure they do not become burdens to others? Help participants identify their daily, weekly, and monthly responsibilities. Some examples are paying bills on time, washing clothes, cleaning their homes, etc. It's when you don't take care of the little things, they can become a burden. An example is not paying your electric bill, which leads to having your electricity turned off. Participants need to take care of the daily things so they don't become burdens to others.

Slide 17

Remind participants that Words of Wisdom (WOW) are in Section 7 of their workbooks.

Slide 18

Plan Ahead

Participants who are working NEED to develop a plan to deal with unexpected things. This will help them stabilize their incomes. An important part of work is to be a reliable employee.

Slide 19

Here is a normal day overview. Remember not to get distracted by sharing stories.

Slide 20

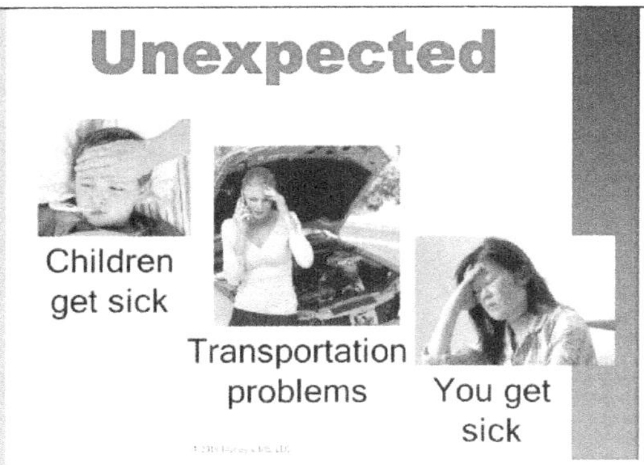

Here is an unexpected day they may need to plan for. The next discussion will have them think of what they could do about the unexpected so they don't lose their jobs.

Slide 21

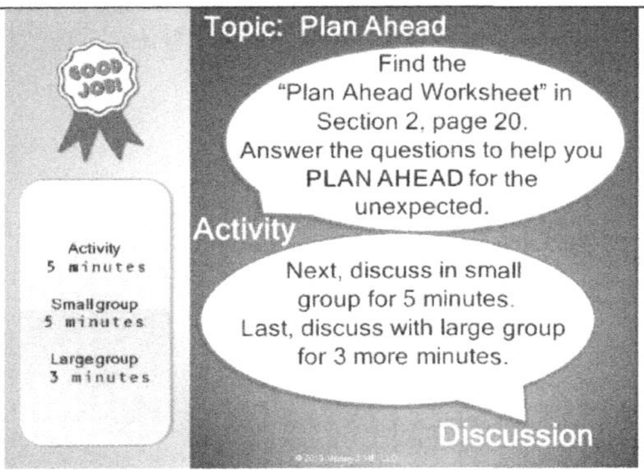

Have the participants start working on their Plan Ahead Worksheets? Have them share with the group. If participants are not working for their income, have them discuss how they could help someone who does have a job keep their job. Could they help babysit if needed, offer a ride, etc.? How much better is it when we work in community to help each other when needed.

Slide 22

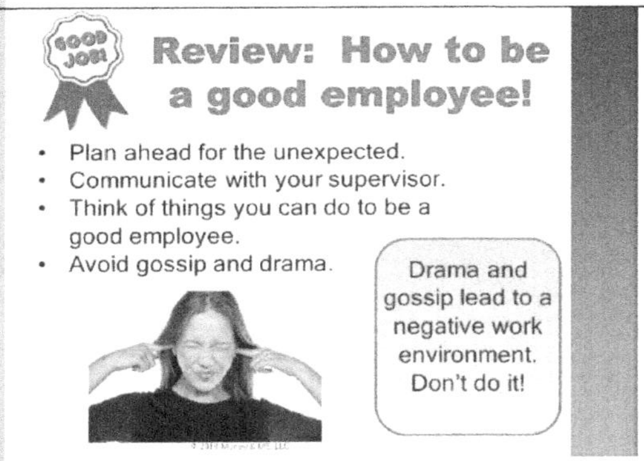

After the discussion, this slide will review some of the key points that should have been discussed. One of the biggest problems in a workplace is gossip. Encourage participants to stay out of drama and gossip!

Slide 23

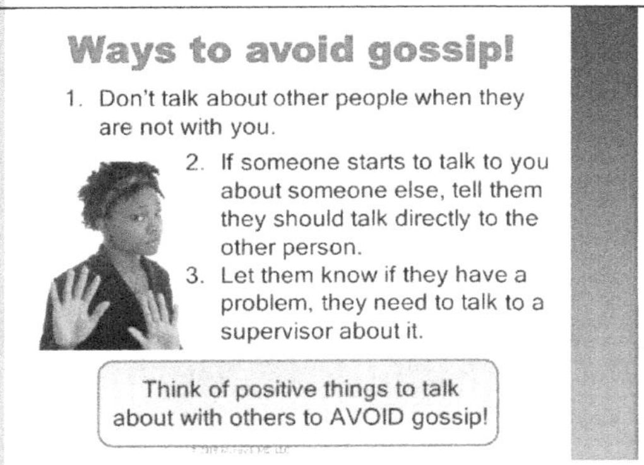

This slide is to give practical advice on avoiding gossip. Gossip can be very harmful to families and work environments. Encourage participants to think of positive things to talk about with others to avoid gossip.

Slide 24

This slide is a LOT of fun and is very impactful. Raise your hand when you ask, "Who would like to have $365 one year from today?" Wait for everyone's hands to go up! This is reinforcing how much daily spending is costing them per year.

Slide 25

This visual says it all. They would have $365 if they saved $1.00 every day for a year.

Slide 26

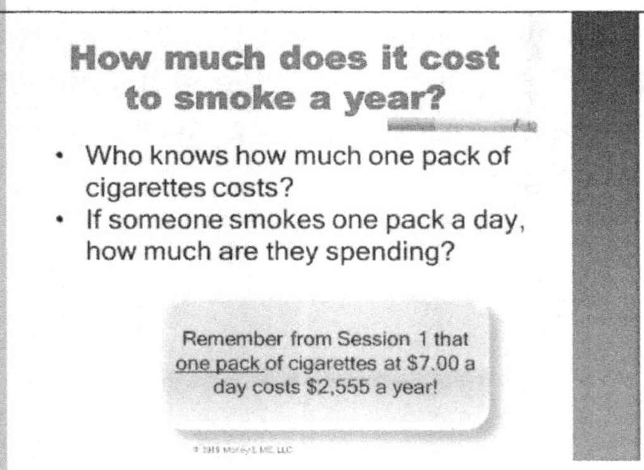

Ask participants how much a pack of cigarettes costs? DO NOT ASK WHO SMOKES!

Slide 27

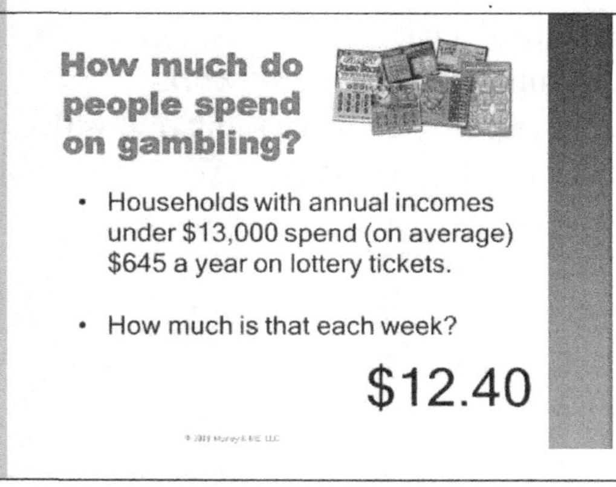

This statistic is from Casino Watch. Visit www.marketoracle.co.uk/Article14128.html

Slide 28

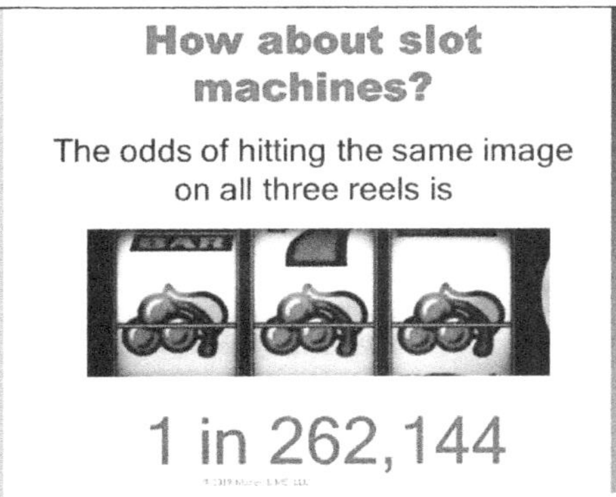

This statistic is according to "How Slot Machines Work" by Tom Harris, at the howstuffworks website.

Slide 29

A lot of participants think gambling is the answer to their money problems. They don't realize the chances of winning are extremely slim. If they know someone who won, or if they have won, what did they do with their winnings? More often than not, they probably gambled again.

Slide 30

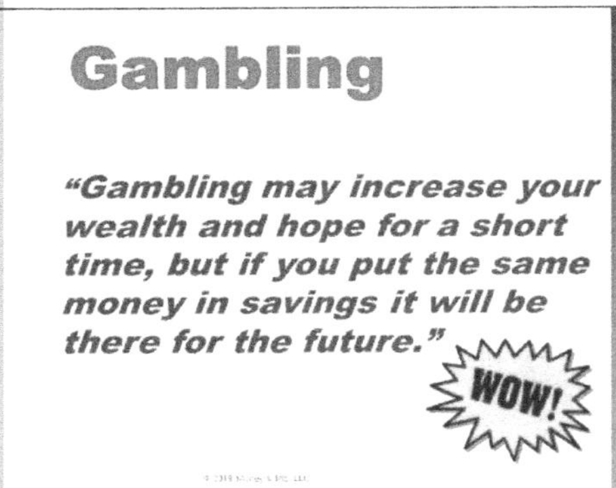

Gambling is common in the low-income culture. We do not want to encourage participants to gamble.

Slide 31

Money & ME does not condone gambling. However, many of the participants are already gambling. You are just guiding them into the realization of how much money it can cost. We are relating gambling to an entertainment activity because, for many of them it starts as entertainment. However, it may develop into an addiction.

Slide 32

Entertainment costs can add up very quickly. This slide illustrates how much money movies can cost.

Slide 33

This gives some ideas on ways to watch movies without spending so much money.

Slide 34

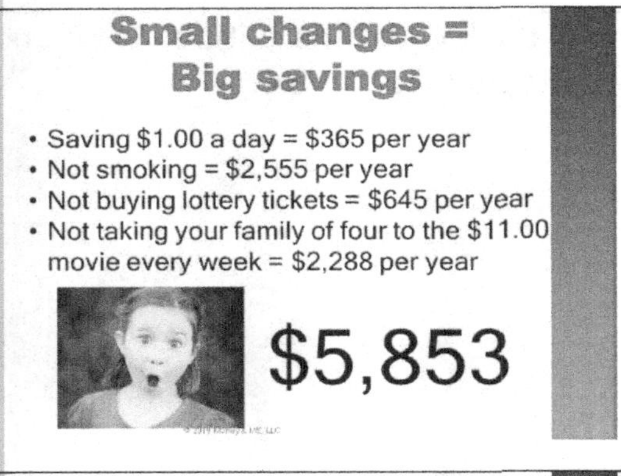

It is good for participants to see how little changes can equal big savings.

Slide 35

Saver OR Spender?

Helping people identify if they are a saver or a spender will help them get in control of their money. This activity will have them look at their parents' spending behaviors and who they identify with. **Trainer Story: Share a story about how your parents handled money or how they taught you to handle money.**

Slide 36

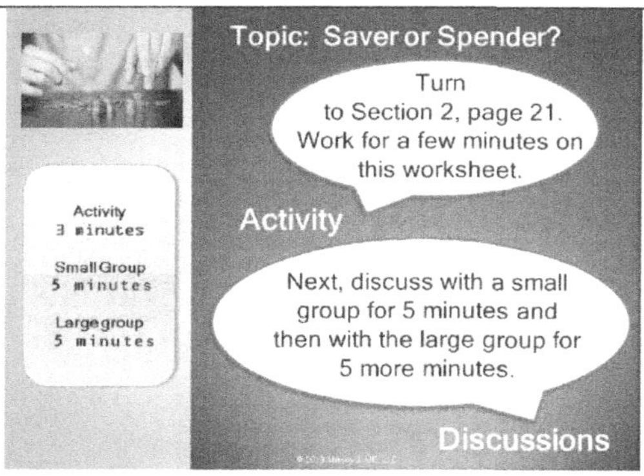

Discovering how their parents handled money will offer great insight into how they themselves are handling money. Which of their parents was the spender or saver? Did they know if there would be food on the table at night? Are they now living on welfare? This is bringing out information about the past, present, and future. They could be in generational poverty.

Slide 37

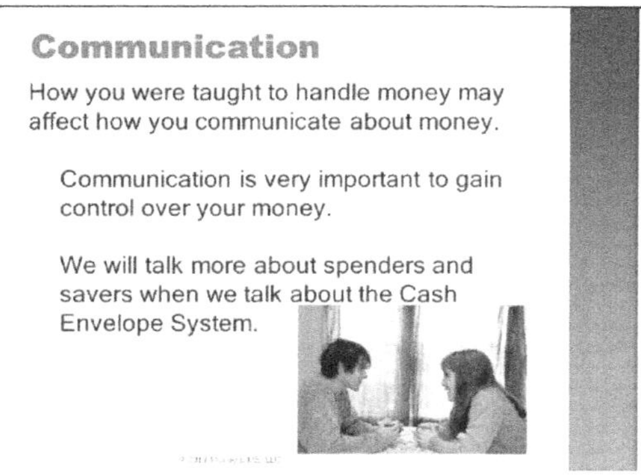

Communication

Talking about how family members spend money can be a very sensitive topic as well as a HUGE source of conflict. There will be more discussion on this topic during the workshop. THIS IS EXTREMELY IMPORTANT. Remember, you are planting a seed that could bring families back together.

Slide 38

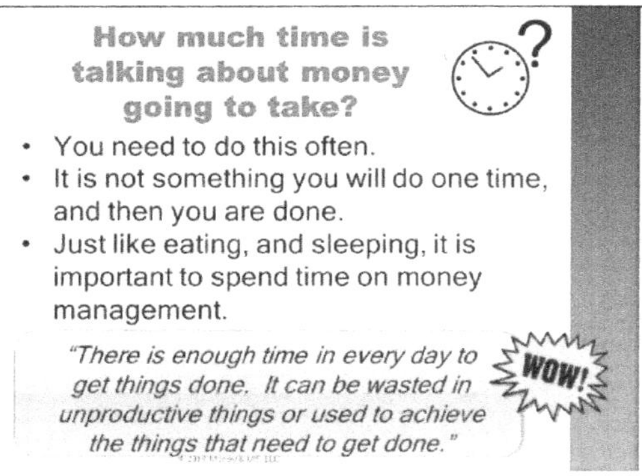

It is important for participants to realize gaining control over their money is going to take some time. It is not something they do once and then never do again. At the workshop, we will talk about writing down all of their spending, or recording it in an app. Completing a calendar of when they get paid and when their bills are due will also take time. Let them know it is worth it!

Slide 39

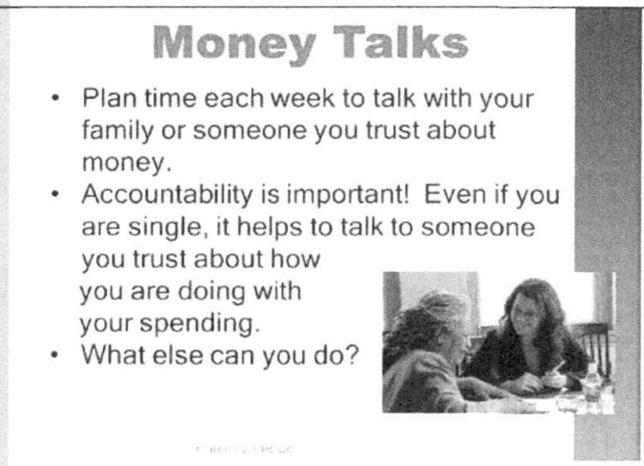

Getting families and / or singles to communicate on a regular basis about money issues is critical. Good communication will help them with their financial plan and help reach their goals. Encourage them to keep communication open by not blaming one another. This can be VERY difficult to do. Accountability to another person is also a very important part of handling money issues.

Slide 40

Changing Habits

Slide 41

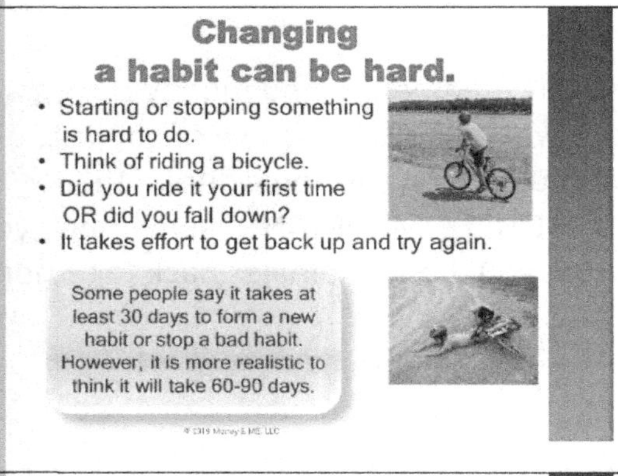

Changing a habit IS very hard. Participants need to understand even if they fail at first, they should keep trying. It can take up to 90 days to change a habit.

Slide 42

These slides are leading up to the next discussion group.

Slide 43

Save discussion for the upcoming activity slide.

Slide 44

It is important to understand why people continue to do things they know are unhealthy for them. Identifying the "why" will help them make changes.
Trainer Story: Think of an unhealthy habit you once had. When did you realize it was unhealthy and how did you change it?

Slide 45

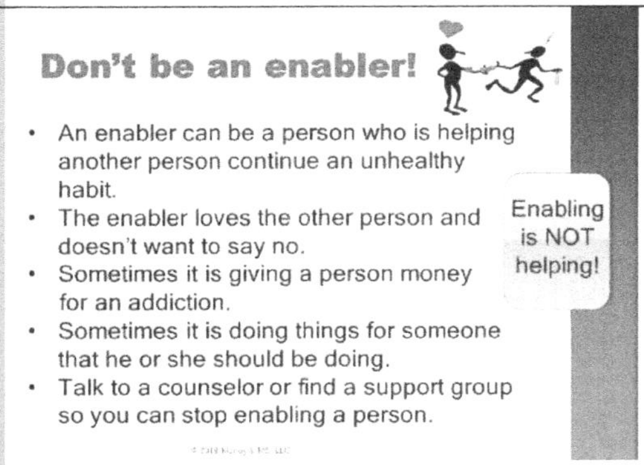

Sometimes a person may be enabling another person's negative behavior or addiction. Encourage them to get some help so they can stop.

Slide 46

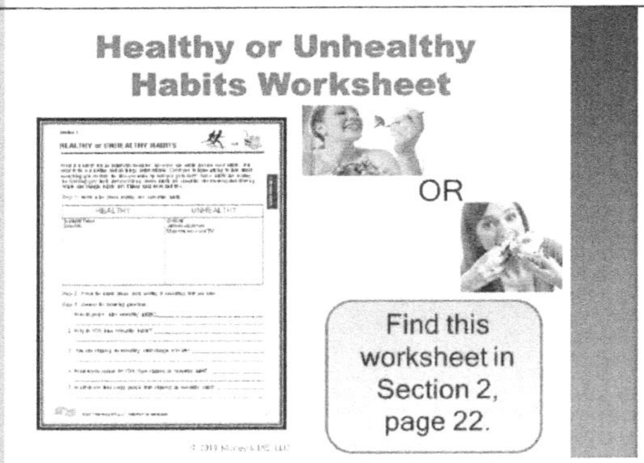

Have the participants turn to Section 2 of the workbook and find the Healthy or Unhealthy Habits Worksheet.

Slide 47

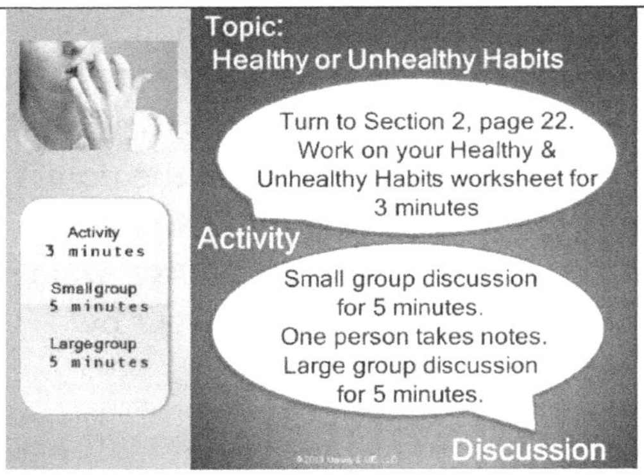

Once again, DO NOT skip the discussion activities. This is where REAL learning takes place. Encourage participants to share what they have learned.
Allow 13 minutes for this activity and discussion.

Session 3: Smart Shopping

Slide 1

Slide 2

Smart Shopper Ideas
The purpose of this section is to show different ways people can save money through smart shopper ideas.

Slide 3

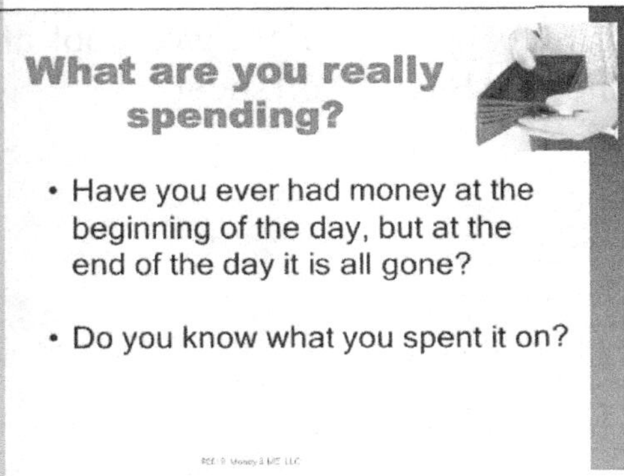

It is easy to lose track of where your money is going. It is often hard to remember what you spent your money on. This is why writing it down is so important.

Slide 4

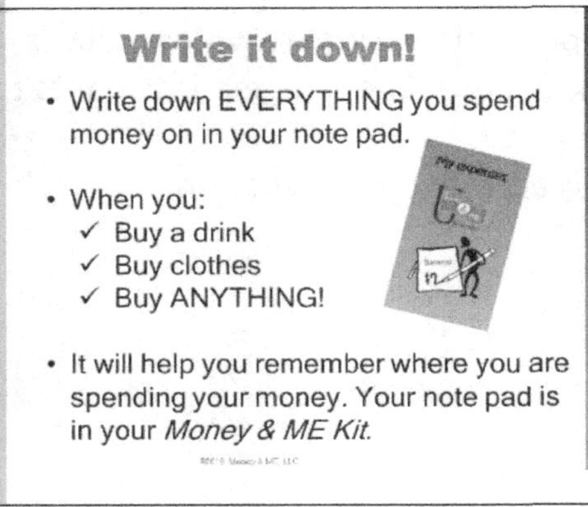

Take out your note pad from the plastic accordion. Ask participants to find theirs. Let them know their note pads are VERY important in managing their money. They need to start writing down EVERYTHING they spend in the note pads. It is hard to remember to do this, but it will help them understand where their money is going. As a Trainer, you should also do this so you can talk about your own experience of writing things down.

Slide 5

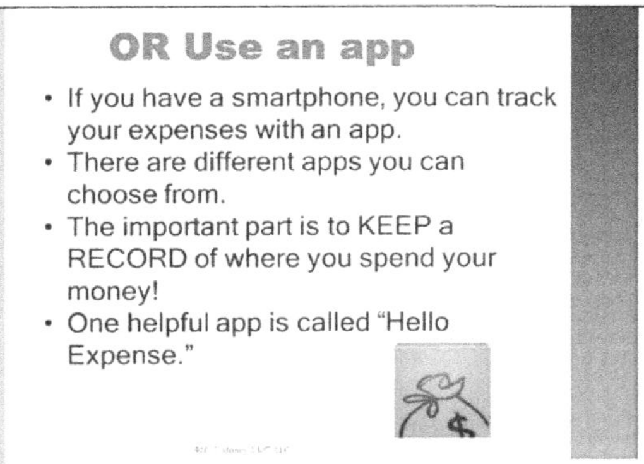

There are a LOT of apps for people to use to help them with their spending. If the participants have a smartphone, they can use this instead of a note pad to record their expenses. The important thing is that they are recording what they spend.

Slide 6

Cleaning Recipes. There are three ingredients that participants can buy with their food stamp money to make cleaning products. They are lemon juice, white vinegar, and baking soda. Recipes for homemade cleaning products are in Section 3 of their *Money & ME Workbooks*.

Slide 7

Encourage participants to think "outside the box." Teach them to think of new ways to save money, such as making their own laundry soap. Doing laundry can be so expensive that sometimes people have disposable clothing. They don't clean their clothes, they just go get new ones.

Slide 8

Participants receiving food stamps cannot buy cleaning products with their food stamps. However, they can buy the ingredients to make their own cleaning products.

Slide 9

This is a very simple and practical tip. Encourage participants to look around their homes to see what other things they can cut in half to save money.

Slide 10

Have FUN with this series of slides. Participants get really excited and want to share LOTS of stories. You NEED to maintain control of the class to get through these slides. This information is helping to build trust between the Trainer AND participants. Breaking down trust barriers at the beginning will help the class trust you when we discuss more complicated subjects such as Money Owed and the Payment Plan.

Slide 11

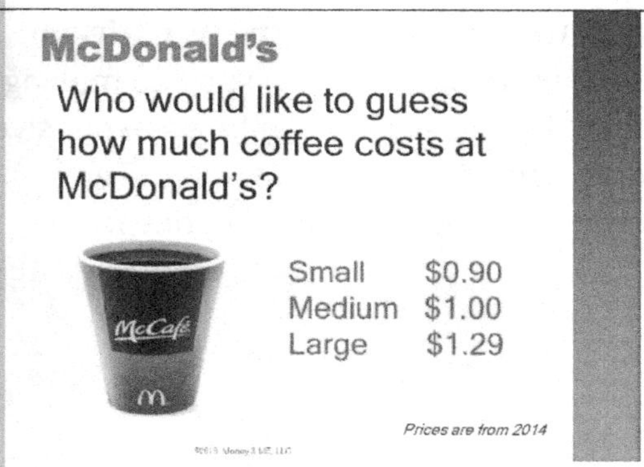

Keep this brief. Prices are from 2014.

Slide 12

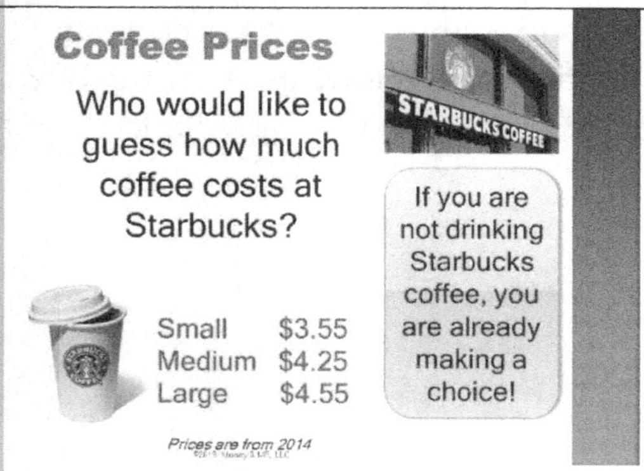

Keep this brief. Most of the participants do NOT buy coffee at Starbucks. The important thing is for them to start realizing they are already making choices about spending money.
Prices are from 2014.

Slide 13

Encourage people to make coffee at home to save money. Prices are from 2014.

Slide 14

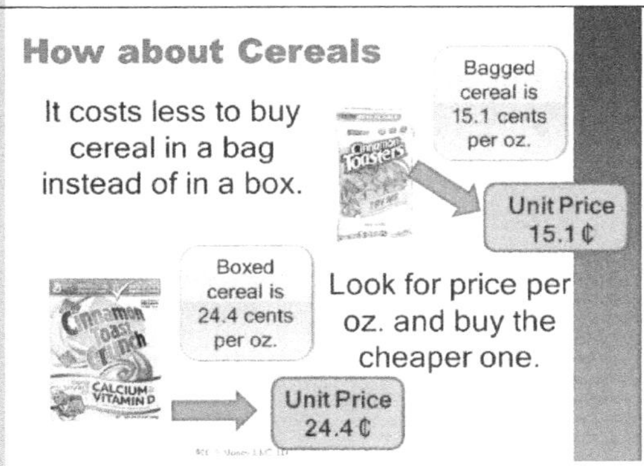

Keep this brief. It will be really fun for you as a Trainer, to see the "light bulb" turn on when participants realize they should look at the "price per oz." instead of the total price. Prices are from 2014.

Slide 15

Here are more examples of the increased cost of price per oz.

Slide 16

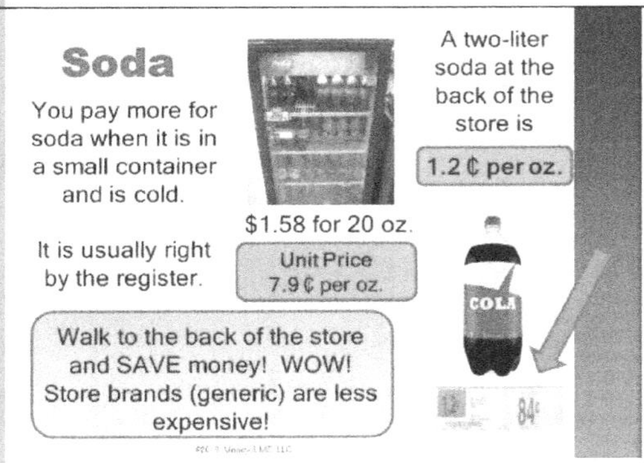

Participants will start to see they can make money-saving choices as simple as buying their soda at the BACK of the store.
Prices are from 2014.

Slide 17

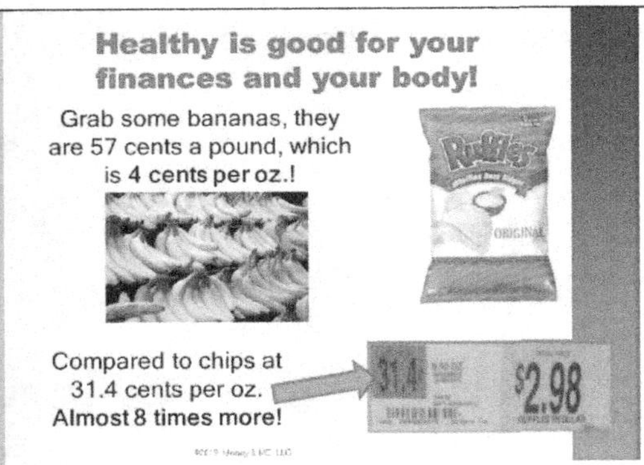

Keep this brief. Prices are from 2014.

Slide 18

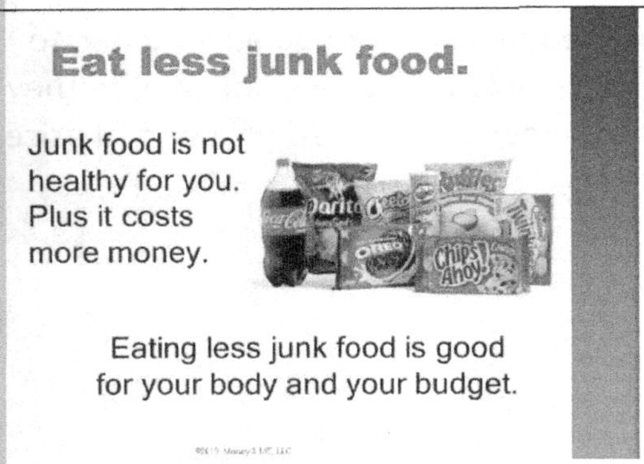

One *Money & ME* participant stopped renting movies and buying chips and soda at the convenience store. This young woman started saving over $300 per month by using smart shopping tips and making better choices.

Slide 19

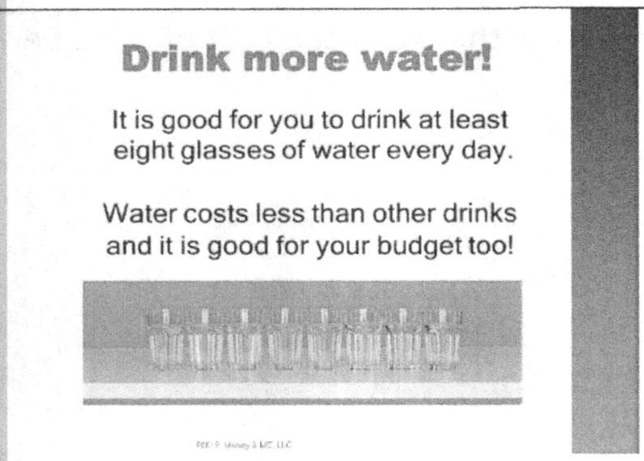

NOTE: Depending upon a person's size, this amount may change.

Slide 20

Point out that both plates have small portions of starchy foods, large portions of fruits and veggies, and small meat portions. One plate is divided, the other is an example of combining starchy foods, fruits or vegetables, and meat into one dish. Both of these pictures show meals the participants can make.

Slide 21

The concept of buying ingredients and cooking at home may be new to some participants.

Slide 22

Trainers use a timer. This is a fun game to challenge people to think of different recipes with one ingredient. Encourage the group to write down answers. Share ideas after each food item.

Slide 23

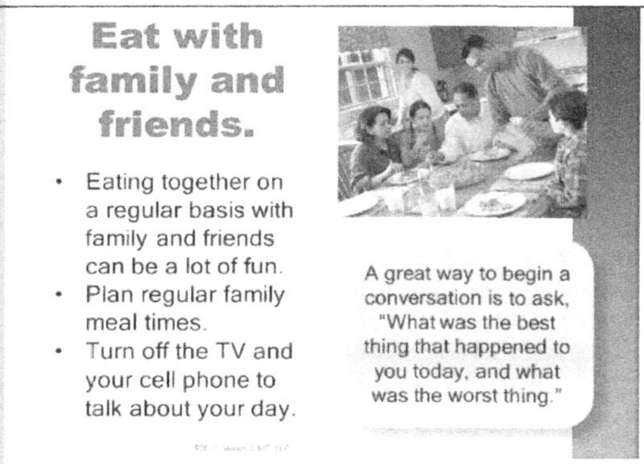

Eating with people is a great way to build relationships. Encourage participants with families to eat together. Single people can get together with friends and share a meal. Potlucks are a great way for people to get together without the burden being on one person to provide the entire meal. A fun thing to do for a person's birthday is think of a positive memory of that person and share it at a birthday dinner.

Slide 24

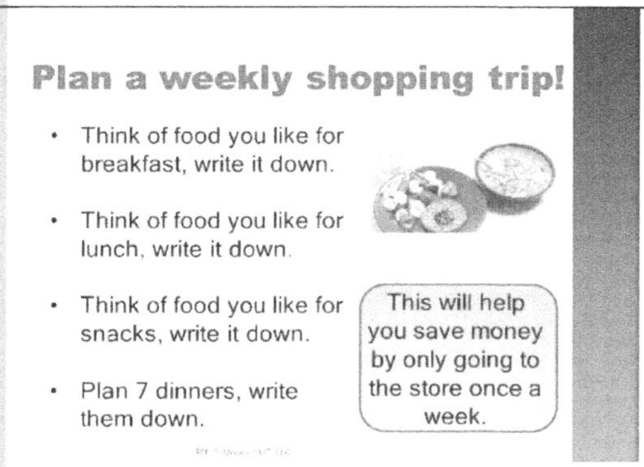

Meal Planning / Cooking at Home

It is important for participants to start planning their meals ahead of time so they will only go to the grocery store one time per week.

Slide 25

Meal planning is designed to be a non-threatening discussion, especially for families who are trying to improve communication. This discussion allows participants to learn from each other and bridge the gap to talk about more difficult topics later in the workshop.
This is a good place for a 5-minute break.

Slide 26

These slides can generate a FUN discussion. Remember you NEED to maintain control of the class and WATCH YOUR TIME when sharing stories.

Slide 27

There are great deals on clothing and other items at thrift stores at a fraction of the cost of department store prices.

Slide 28

Here are two great websites for people who are "Outfit Challenged." One is Missussmartypants.com and another is Pinterest.com.

Slide 29

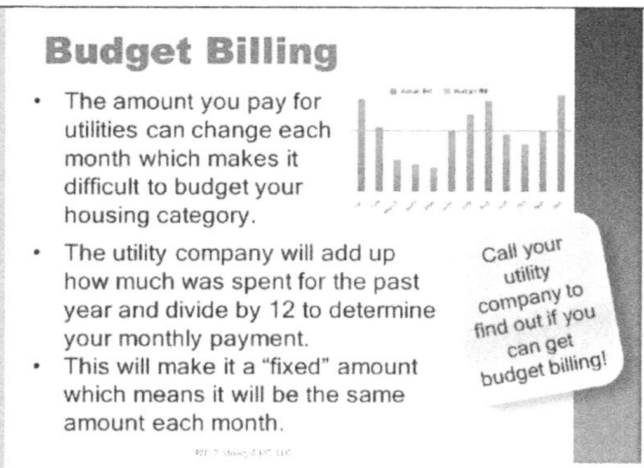

Encourage participants to call their utility companies to see if they are eligible for budget billing. Usually they will need to have been paying on time. Budget billing will make it easier for participants to budget their housing expenses.

Slide 30

Habitat for Humanity is a national non-profit that helps low-income people buy homes. Encourage participants who would like more information to call. In Albuquerque, participants can get a 3-bedroom, 2-bathroom, 2 car garages for approximately $450/month mortgage payment.

Slide 31

This is going to be hard for some participants to hear. Some do not have insurance and this reminds them of something they should be doing and they are not. This could be a good money goal.

Slide 32

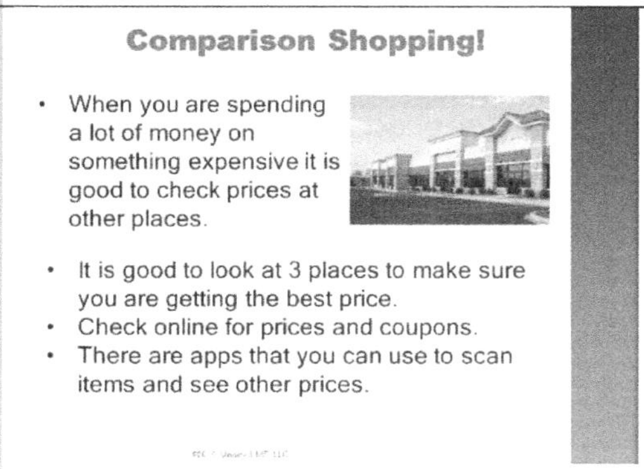

Encourage participants to check around for prices. They can make choices about where they shop and how much they want to spend.

Slide 33

Many stores have different prices online than they do in their stores. Best Buy is one example. Encourage participants to look at online pricing before they spend their money.

Slide 34

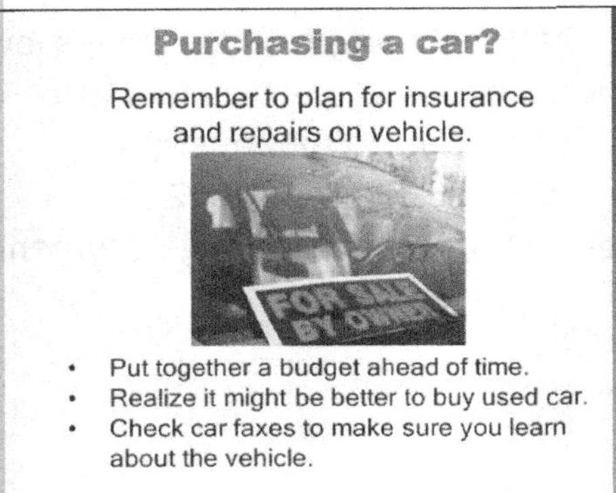

There are additional costs when purchasing a vehicle. This includes insurance and maintenance on vehicles. It is important to remember that when looking at how much a person can afford to spend on a vehicle. It is also important to check the vehicle ahead of time to learn the history of the vehicle.

Slide 35

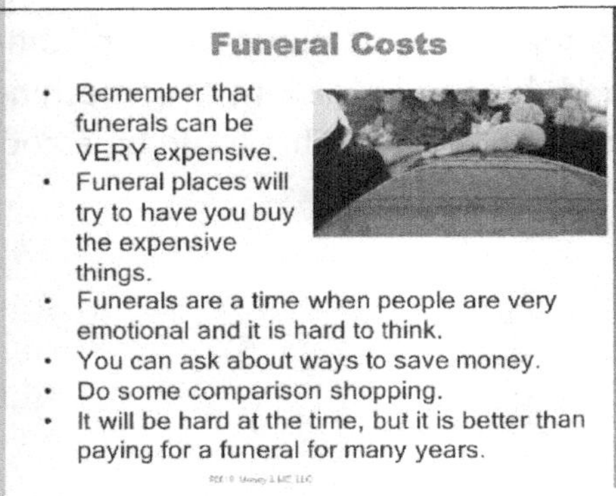

Funerals are a very emotional time, and funeral homes can offer the most expensive options. It is important for participants to understand that they do have choices. It is good for them to ask for other options and shop around.

Slide 36

Here are more ideas of ways to save money. Ask participants if they are familiar with Craigslist where they can purchase used items at reduced cost. Many times, low-income people are purchasing from "Rent to Own" stores and spending more money than they need to.

Slide 37

This is a quick review. Keep this brief.

Slide 38

Feelings Affect Spending

Feelings ABSOLUTELY affect spending habits and it is important for participants to understand this. They may start to realize they are really spending money because of how they feel.

Slide 39

Feeling happy about an event can cause people to spend too much money. Participants should budget for celebrations to keep them spending money they don't have.

Slide 40

Participants should think about their relationship with money.

Slide 41

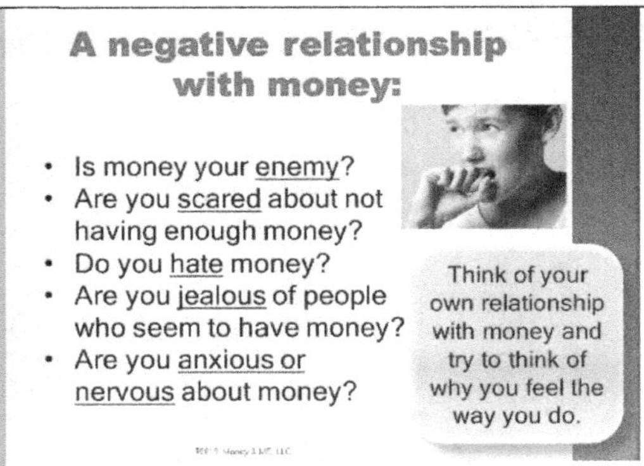

Many people may have negative feelings about money. They need to learn to identify these feelings.

Slide 42

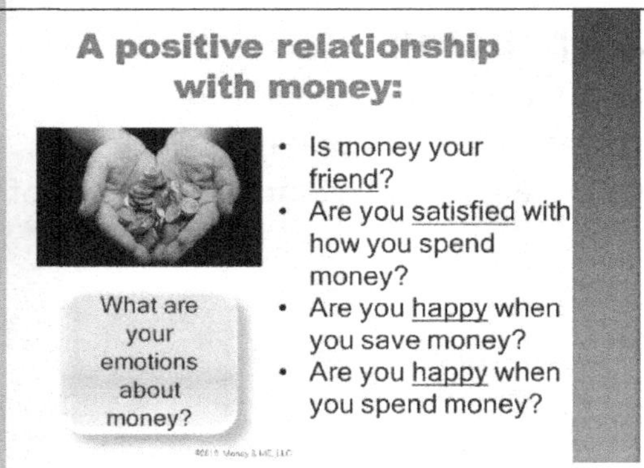

People can have a positive relationship with money. It is important to identify emotions related to saving and spending money.

Slide 43

It is important for participants to realize that they may be spending money because of their emotions or bad habits. There are activities in Section 6 to help people change their habits. There is also a list of activities that people can do for free or very little money. This list is helpful if people are spending money when they are bored.

Slide 44

Let them know they were created for good things.

Slide 45

This slide shows that people who spend more than they make are less happy than those who spend less than they make.

Slide 46

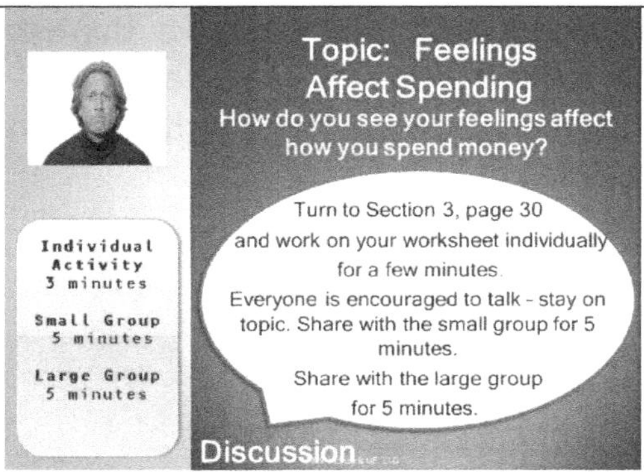

Asking these questions is a great way to help people remember what they did as kids to earn money for things they wanted. Now participants can encourage their children to do the same. Relationship building is being developed among participants, through the discussion, as they realize how much they know.

Slide 47

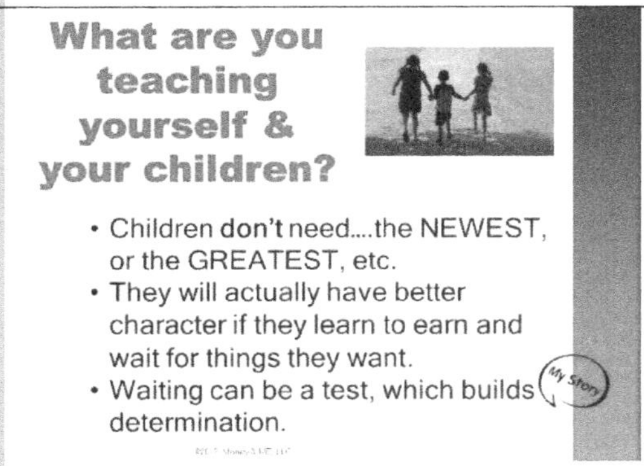

Teaching Children

Look at our society. People have developed a thinking pattern that they are entitled to whatever they want. They expect to have things given to them.

To break this expectation and cycle, we introduce the concept of NOT giving children the newest, latest, greatest, etc. By waiting, they can learn patience and determination.

Trainer Story: Share a story about what you did as a kid to earn extra money. Be brief.

Slide 48

It is good for our children to have small trials and work through them to help them with larger trials in life.

Slide 49

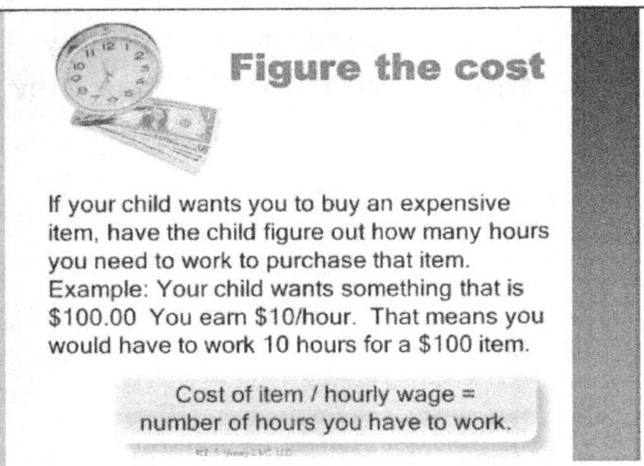

It is important for children to know how hard their parents need to work to purchase items. Having them do the math will help them realize the value of an item.

Slide 50

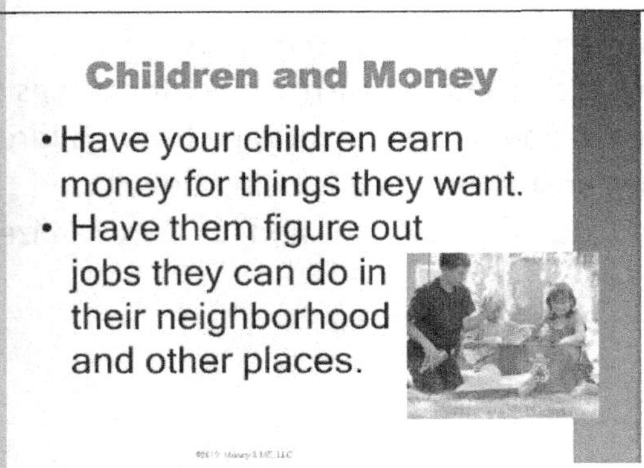

Earning money for items children want will teach them to appreciate things more and maybe have a better work ethic. This is encouraging participants to help their children take responsibility for themselves.

Slide 51

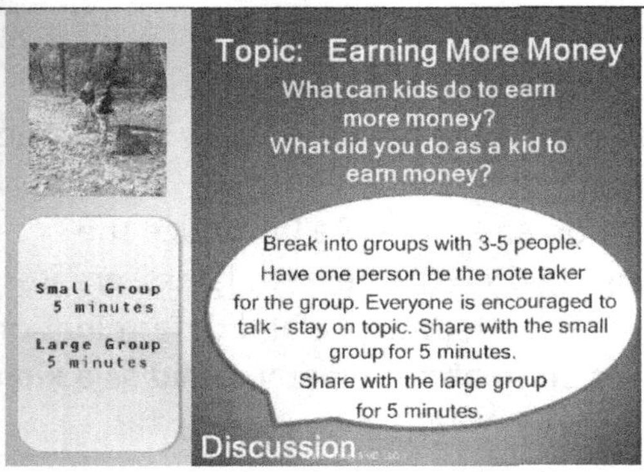

Asking these questions is a great way to help people remember what they did as kids to earn money for things they wanted. Now participants can encourage their children to do the same. Relationship building is being developed among participants, through the discussion, as they realize how much they know.

Slide 52

Help share success! If it is shopping smarter, not buying soda, or comparison shopping, have people share their success!

Session 4: Plan for Money Owed

Slide 1

Slide 2

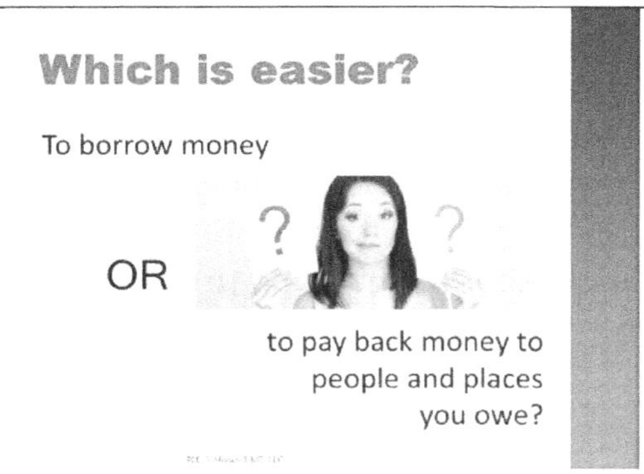

It is important for participants to understand how easy it is to borrow money and how difficult it is to pay it back.

Slide 3

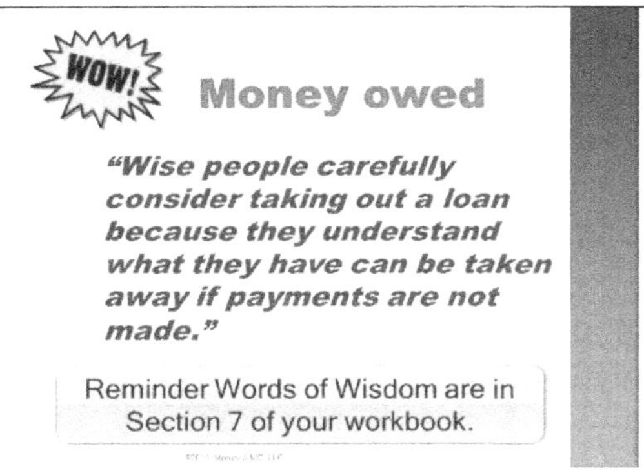

Reminder that Words of Wisdom are found in Section 7 of their workbooks.

Participants may want to co-sign on a loan with someone. It could be to benefit them or someone they know. It is important for them to be VERY cautious about co-signing a loan, even if it is for a family member. If people co-sign and the debt is not paid they could lose their own homes, cars, etc.

Slide 4

Owing money is a burden and can feel like having a huge weight on their shoulders. This slide illustrates how that might feel.

Slide 5

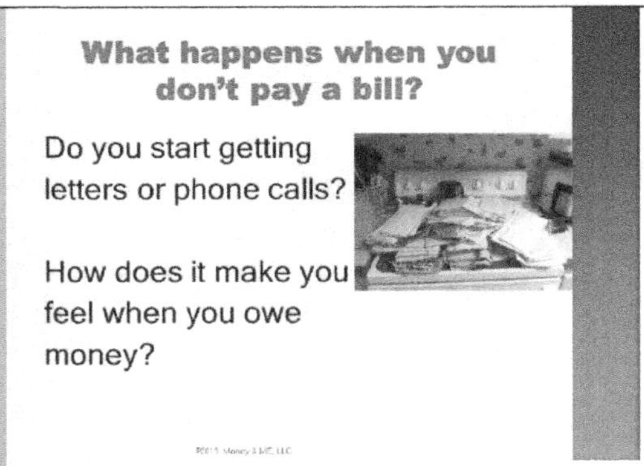

Owing money doesn't feel good. But there is hope. Let them know we will talk about a plan to help them. Paying off money owed doesn't happen right away. However, if they stick to the plan it will work.

Slide 6

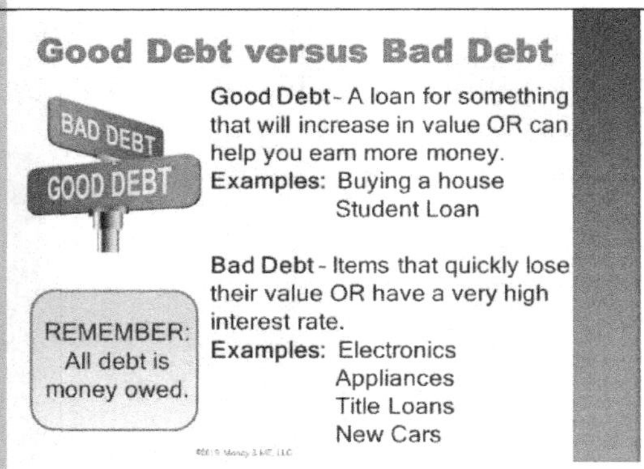

Going into debt over electronics, appliances, furniture, etc. is NOT a good idea. As a Trainer you do NOT want to encourage debt. However, it is worth mentioning student loans. If they are going back to school, a student loan may be an option to help cover the cost of school. Remind them to check out other options for financial aid to pay for school.

Slide 7

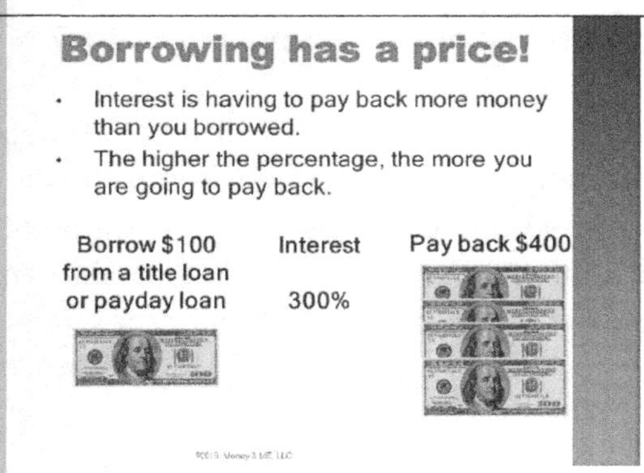

It may surprise you how many people do not understand what interest means. Some are embarrassed to ask, "What is interest?" so they sign papers for loans because they don't want to appear stupid.

DO NOT get into a long discussion about interest. KEEP THIS SIMPLE!

All participants need to know is they are paying back more money than they borrowed.

Slide 8

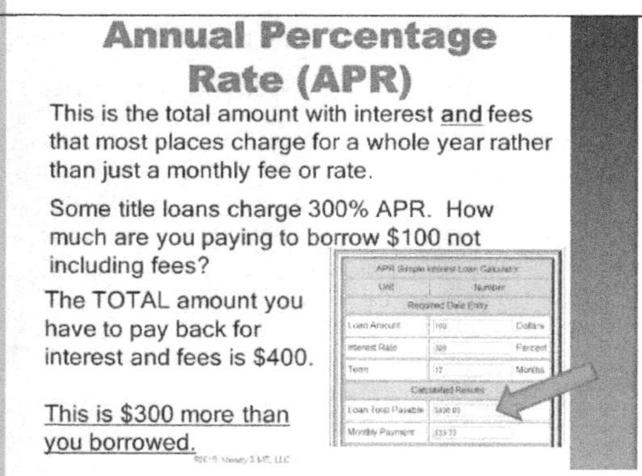

This is as technical as *Money & ME* will get on this topic. Keep it brief. If participants have questions, encourage them to schedule a follow-up session. Questions will start to confuse people.

Slide 9

Many participants do not realize how much money someone else is getting from them through interest. This may shock some of them. Realizing the amount of interest they may pay could help them make better choices in the future.

Slide 10

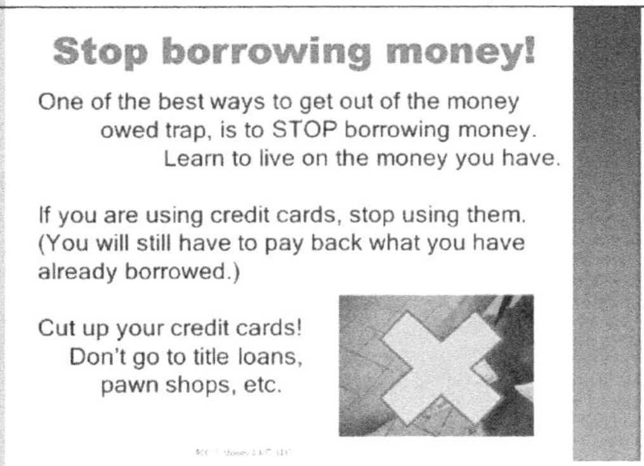

In the middle-class world we say, stop using credit. However, most of our participants typically don't have credit cards or bank loans. They go to pawn shops, payday and title loans, etc. They need to stop this behavior and break the cycle of borrowing money. Remind them about the backpack. Each person is to carry his / her own load so he / she does not become a burden to others. Also, others they are helping need to carry their own loads.

Slide 11

Participants CANNOT afford to have late fees. Talk about how important it is for them to pay bills on TIME, even if they only pay a portion of what they owe.
Examples of bills or loans that might charge late fees: utility companies, medical bills, student loans, etc.

Slide 12

The burden of owing money is very stressful and can lead to health problems. Having a plan to pay off money owed will help alleviate stress.

Slide 13

Money Owed List

This is a transition slide before completing the Money Owed List and making the Payment Plan.

Slide 14

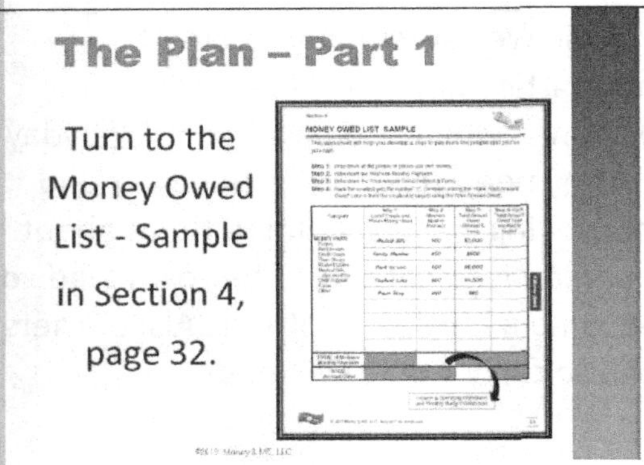

Have participants turn to their Money Owed List Worksheet - Samples.

Slide 15

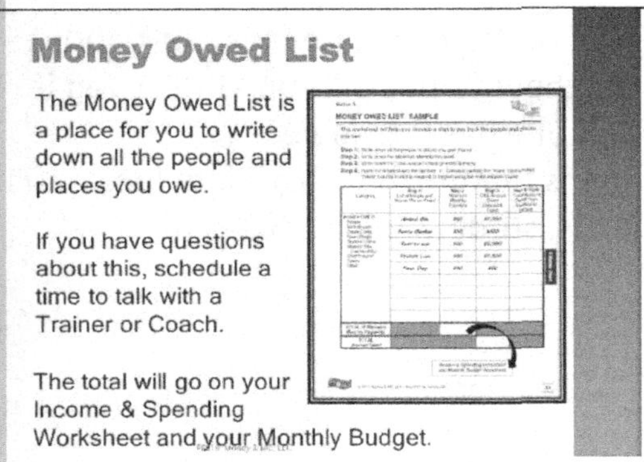

This will help participants complete their Income & Spending Worksheets and the Monthly Budget spending category for Money Owed.

Slide 16

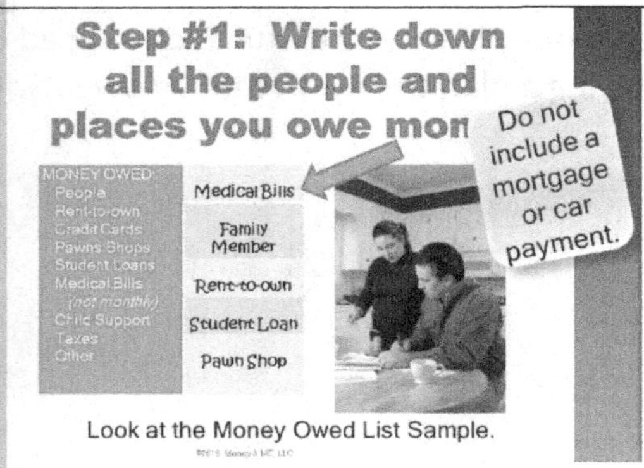

Have participants turn to the Money Owed List Sample Worksheets. They will rank these from the smallest to the greatest as an illustration of how they rank their own Money Owed List.

Slide 17

Each participant needs to write down the Minimum Monthly Payment for each person and place he / she owes people and places owed from smallest to greatest. The total will go on the Income and Spending Worksheet. This concept is taught by Dave Ramsey. It is important for people to have an "emotional win" as soon as possible to keep them encouraged to stick to their Money Owed Plan.

Slide 18

Each participant needs to write down the Total Amount Owed. This is the number he / she will use to rank people and places owed from smallest to greatest.

Slide 19

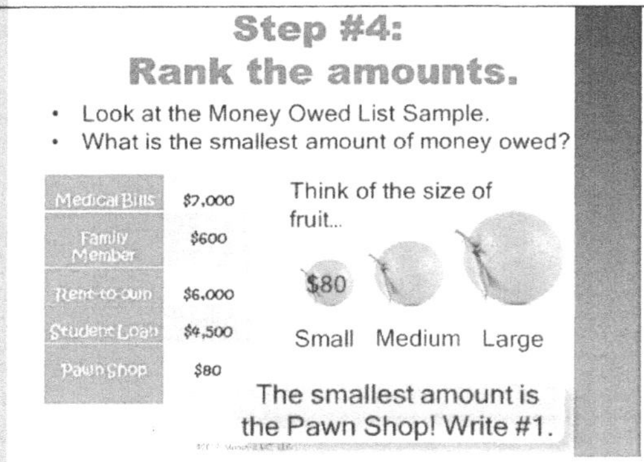

Have participants turn to the Money Owed List Sample Worksheets. They will rank these items from the smallest to the greatest as an illustration of how they will rank their own Money Owed Lists.

Slide 20

Continue to work through the process of ranking the amounts owed with participants.

Slide 21

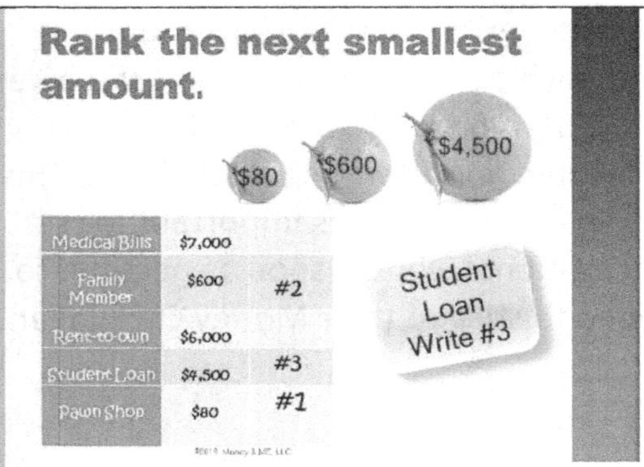

Continue to work through the process of ranking the amounts owed with participants.

Slide 22

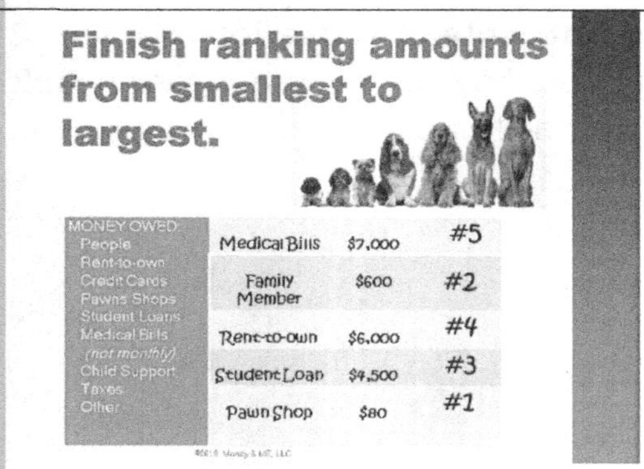

See if the participants can find #4 and #5 on their own. The answers will appear on the screen.

Slide 23

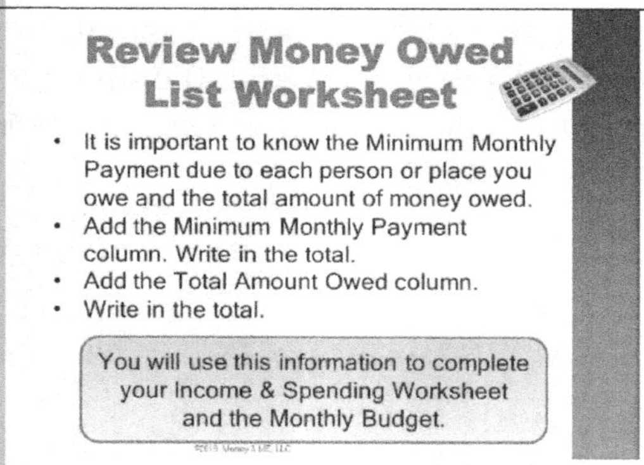

After everything is ranked, they will need to add to find the totals.

Add the Minimum Monthly Payment column.

Add the Total Amount Owed column.

Slide 24

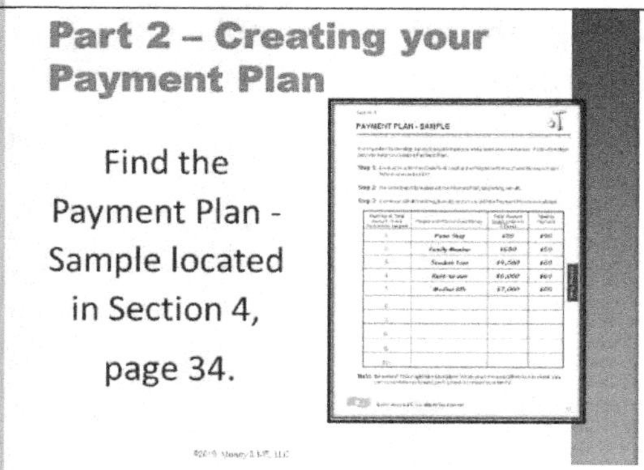

The participants will need to use their blank Payment Plan worksheets and fill in their own amounts of Money Owed.

Slide 25

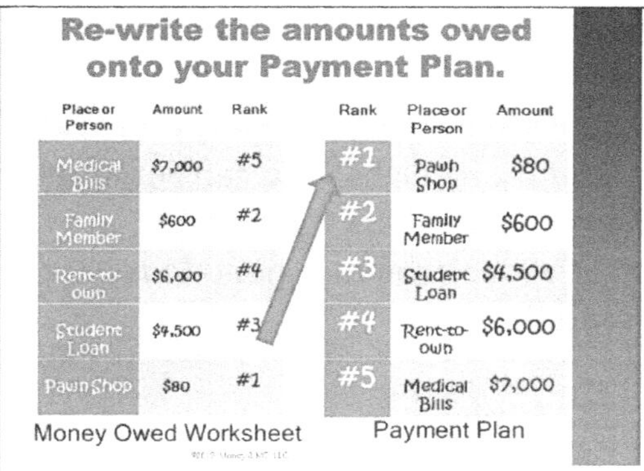

The participants need their Money Owed List Worksheets completed before they can begin their Payment Plans. After participants have listed EVERYTHING they owe, they will rank places or persons from the least amount to the greatest amount. They will use this information to complete their Payment Plans.

Slide 26

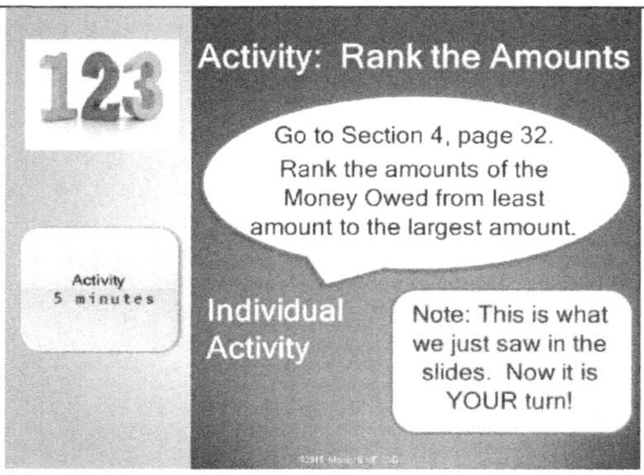

This worksheet reinforces what was shown in the previous slides. This will help them learn to rank the amounts using the Money Owed List – Sample.

Slide 27

The participants need their Money Owed List Worksheets completed before they can begin their Payment Plans. They will need to take their worksheets home to finish. Just have them do what they can remember. Encourage them to schedule a follow-up with a Trainer or Coach.

Slide 28

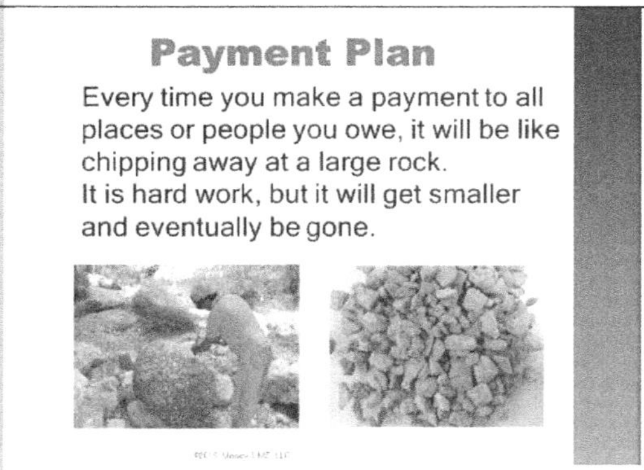

Payment Plan

Paying off money owed is hard work...like chipping away at a rock. We use the analogy to show that it is hard, but every time they make a payment on the money owed, the total amount owed will get smaller. NOTE: The amounts used in the following slides are not exact. They are to show the concept of the Payment Plan.

Slide 29

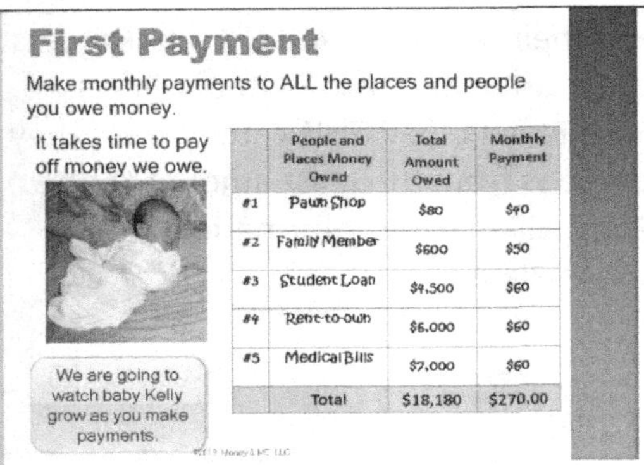

The visuals used are of a baby from birth to six years. It only takes a few moments to go through the slides. It is important for participants to know that paying off money they owe does not happen overnight. You can get into this situation overnight, but it takes years to get out.

Go SLOWLY through the slides. You may need to repeat a slide during the presentation.

Slide 30

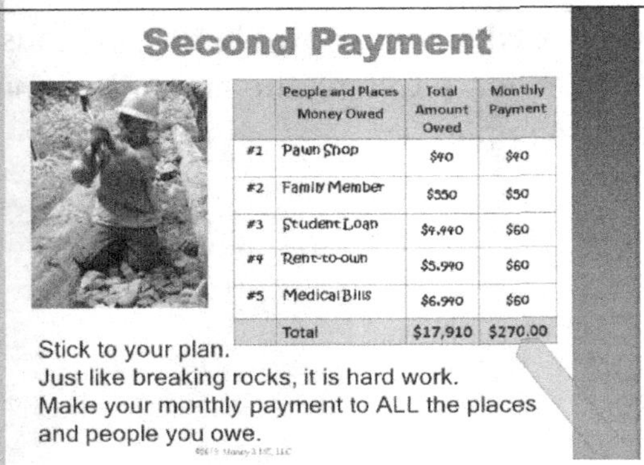

This visual reminds them it takes time and hard work to pay off money they owe.

Slide 31

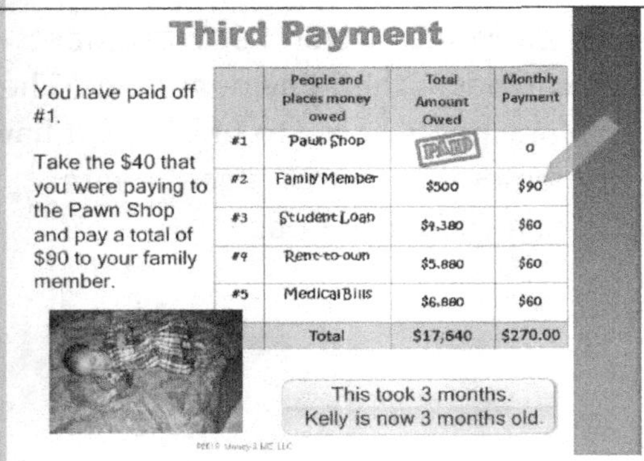

The baby is now three months old. They have paid off one debt. Now they will take the monthly amount of the debt they just paid off and continue that amount to the next debt. This will be their new monthly payments due. They will continue to pay the minimum monthly payment on their other debts.

Slide 32

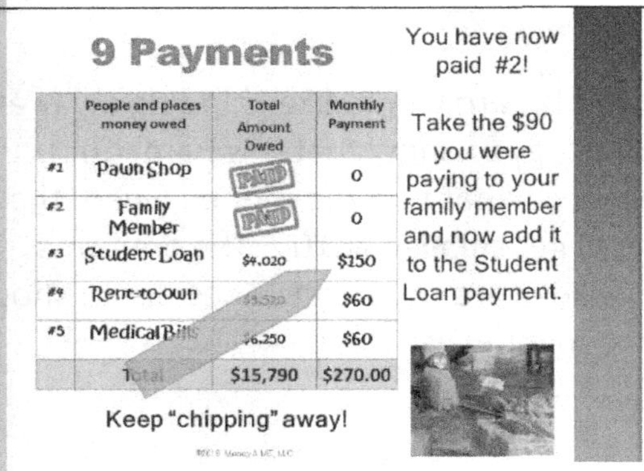

Remember to go SLOWLY through the slides. You may need to repeat a slide during the presentation.

REMINDER: The amounts used in the Payment Plan slides are not exact because interest is not part of the numbers shown. The slides are to show the concept of the Payment Plan.

Slide 33

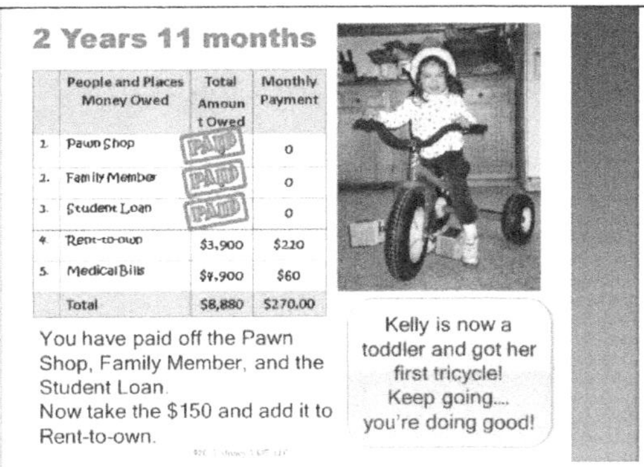

Almost three years! It can happen. Encourage them to keep going.

Slide 34

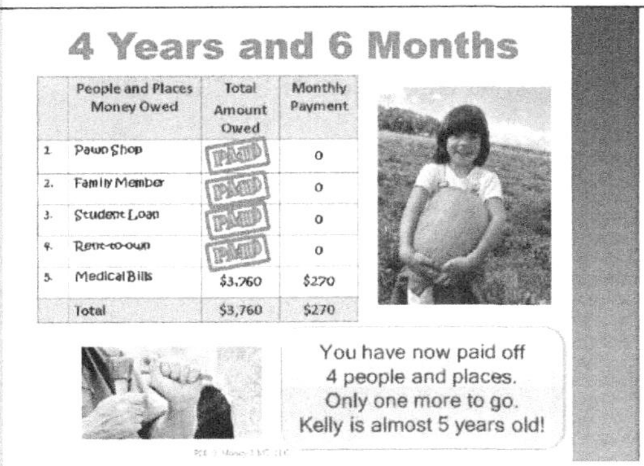

Stay positive.

Slide 35

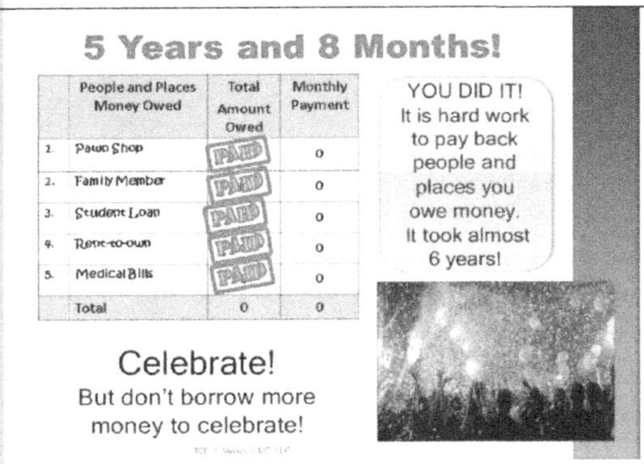

Celebrate, but don't go borrow money again!

Slide 36

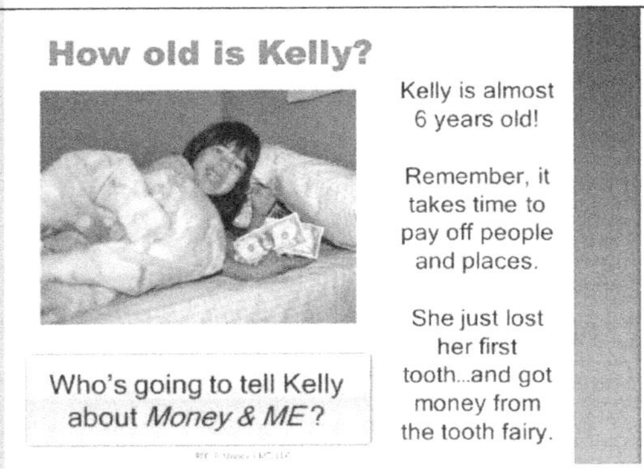

Look how much Kelly has grown! She is almost 6 years old. It is important for participants to understand that it can take a long time to pay back money owed.

Slide 37

This is a review of how to make their Payment Plans. This will be very encouraging to those who owe money.

Slide 38

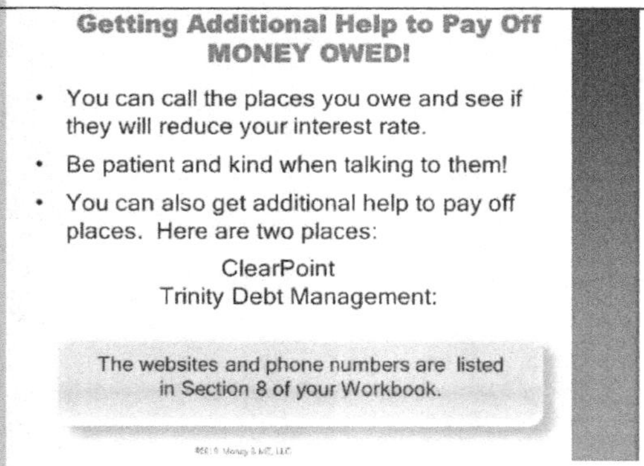

Sometimes the interest rate and process of consolidating debt is difficult. Here are two agencies that can help people.

Slide 39

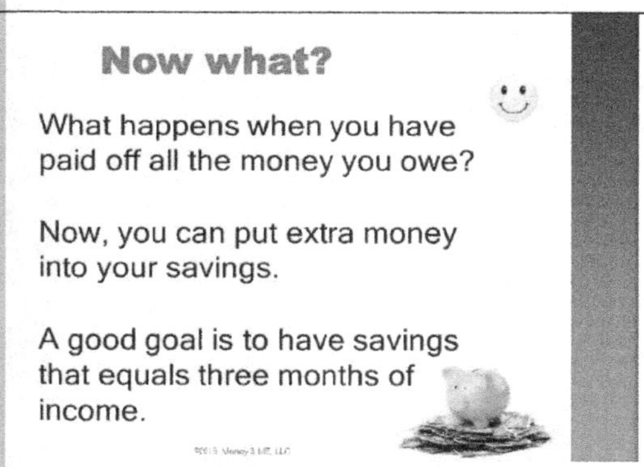

What's next? Once they have paid off the money, they owe they can begin to build their savings!

Slide 40

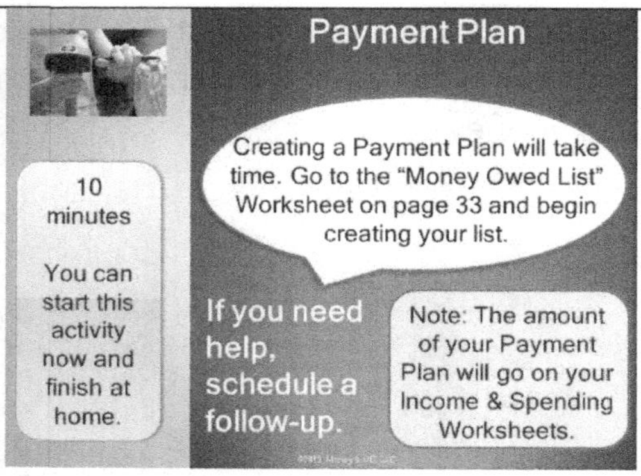

Have participants work on their own Payment Plans at home. The amount they will use is the total from the Minimum Monthly Payment Column listed on the Money Owed List. If participants can pay more than the minimum amount owed, they will finish paying money owed faster. The amount participants can pay each month will be listed in their Income & Spending Worksheets in the Money Owed Category.

Slide 41

Extra Money Plan

This is a transition slide to the next topic "Extra Money Plan."

Slide 42

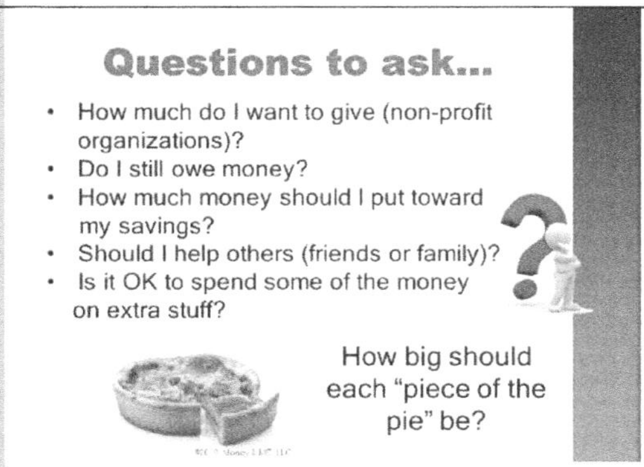

These are very important questions they can ask which will help them make choices about "extra money." Remember as a Trainer, you are guiding them to make decisions for themselves. The picture of a pie is starting to transition them to the concept of a pie chart.

Slide 43

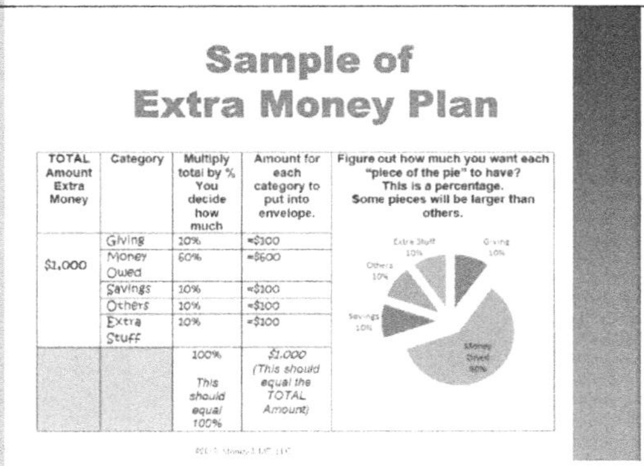

Go slowly. You may need to go over this information a few times if they don't get it right away. This is introducing them to the concept of percentages which can be hard. Let them know there are people who will help them. They just have to decide what size of a "piece of pie" they want each area to get.

Slide 44

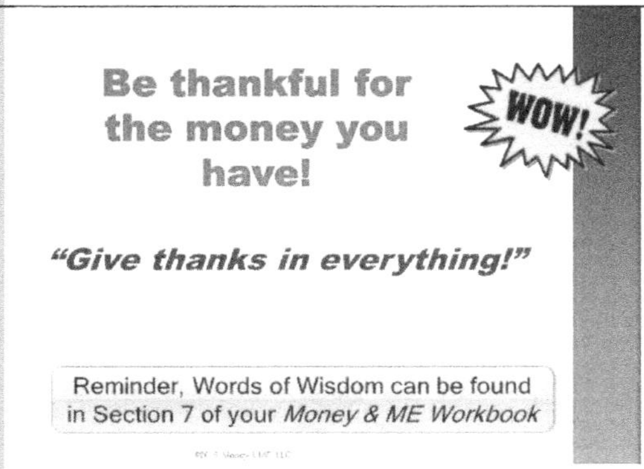

We want them to know they should be thankful for everything they have.

Slide 45

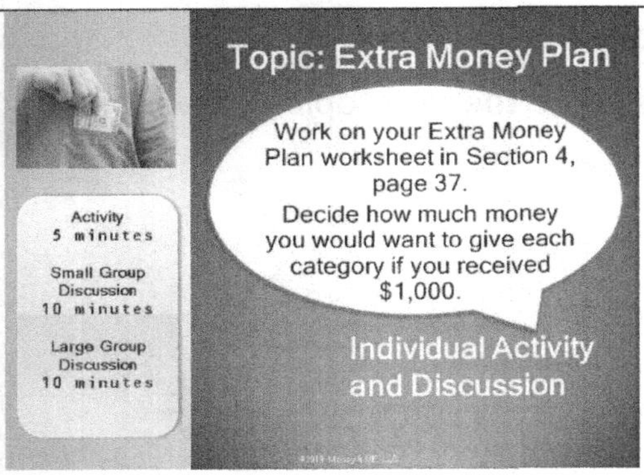

These concepts can help participants make changes that could have a long-lasting impact on their lives. If a person owes money, it can be very depressing and affect other areas of his / her life. Ways to lighten their loads could include planning to save so they do not borrow money.

Slide 46

Boundaries

Establishing healthy boundaries with ourselves and others will help people stick to their budgets.

Slide 47

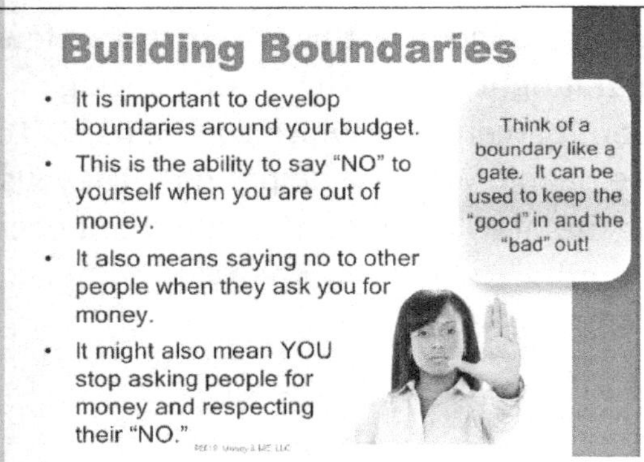

Each person needs to learn self-discipline and say "NO" when they are out of money and tell other people "NO." If a person is always asking others for money, he or she needs to stop.

Slide 48

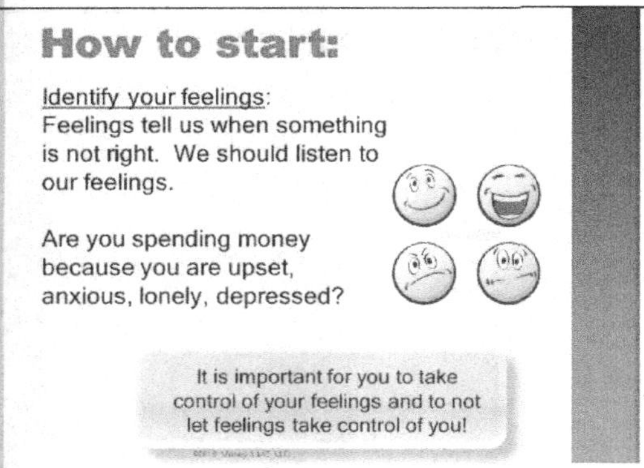

Establishing healthy boundaries with ourselves and others will help people stick to their budgets. Each person needs to learn how to identify their feelings and how it affects their boundaries.

Slide 49

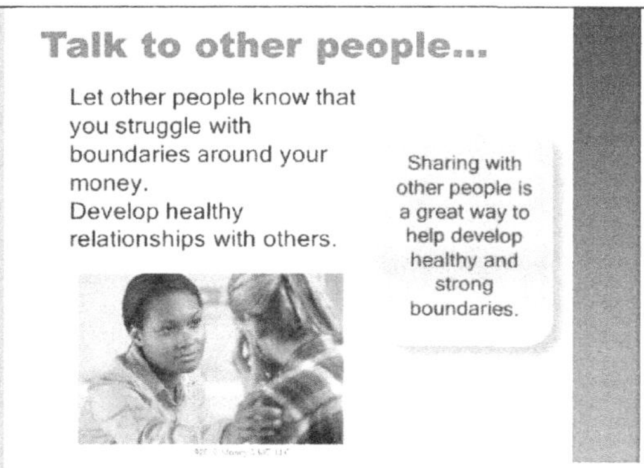

Getting support from other people is critical in establishing healthy boundaries. This is NOT something that can be done individually.

Slide 50

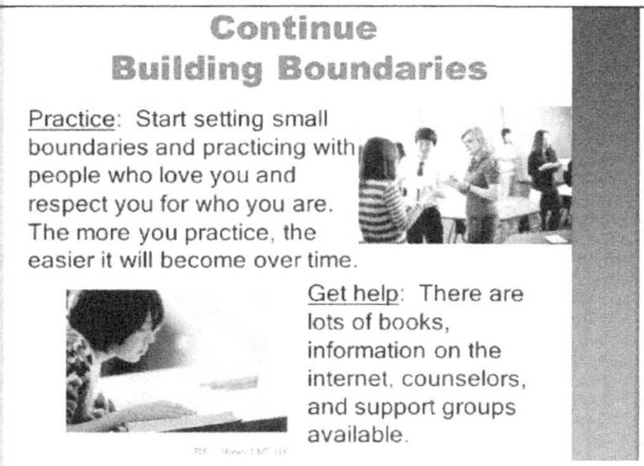

Encourage people who need to work on boundaries to start small and get additional support. This can be through books, information on the internet, counselors, and support groups.

Slide 51

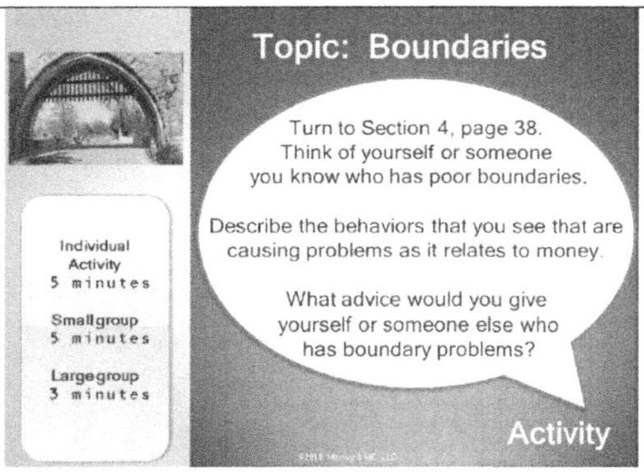

Have participants work on their "Boundaries" worksheets individually for a few minutes. Then they can discuss in small groups and finish in a large group discussion.

Slide 52

Do NOT change the content of this program! Each component was designed specifically for low-income people, tested, and proven to guide them to make changes and take control of their money. By changing the content, you are cheating someone from receiving the full benefit. We welcome your feedback. You may e-mail Contactus@MoneyandME.cash.

Session 5: Build a Budget

Slide 1

Slide 2

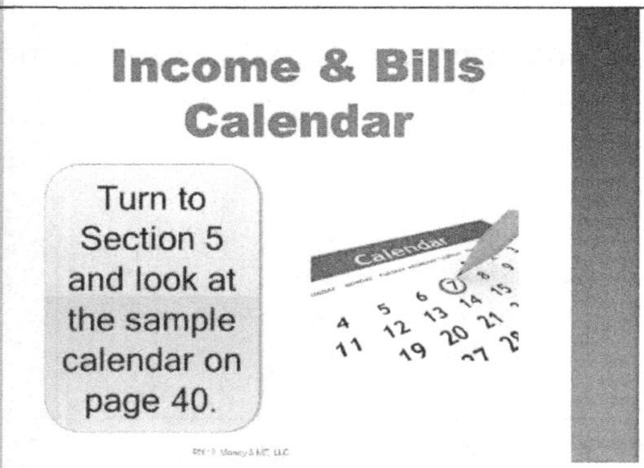

Calendars are helpful when building a budget. A very important part of a budget is knowing when money is coming in and when bills need to be paid. It is important for participants to pay their bills on time so they can avoid late fees.

Slide 3

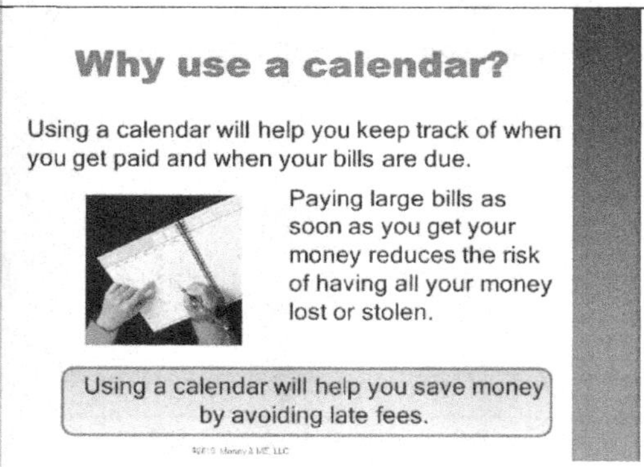

Here are possible benefits of using a calendar.

Slide 4

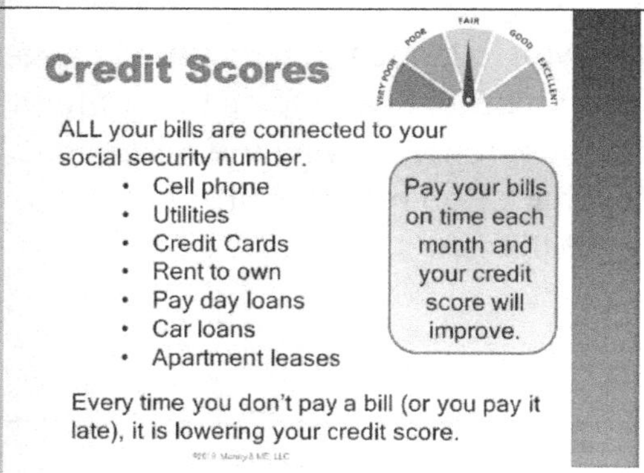

It is important for participants to understand that every time they pay a bill, or don't pay a bill, it is impacting their credit scores.

Slide 5

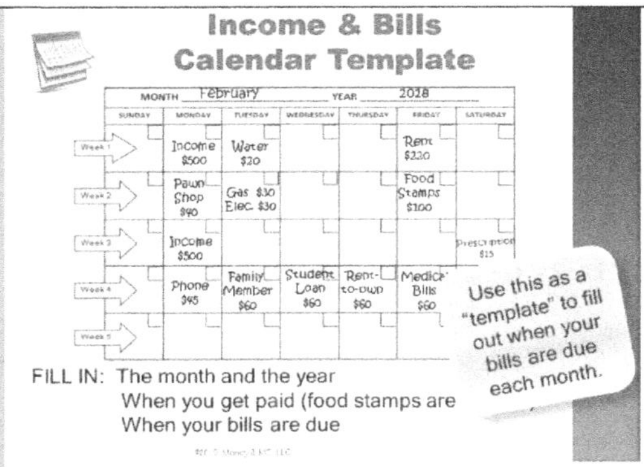

Teach participants to begin writing down on a calendar when they get paid and when their bills are due. This will help them gain control over their money. Remember MOST participants are living on approximately $1,000/month. Remind them the Income & Bills Calendar is located in Section 4 of their *Money & ME Workbook.*

Slide 6

It is important for participants to learn how to use a calendar app if they have the app on their phone. It is good for them to set it as a recurring event so it will help them each month pay bills on time.

Slide 7

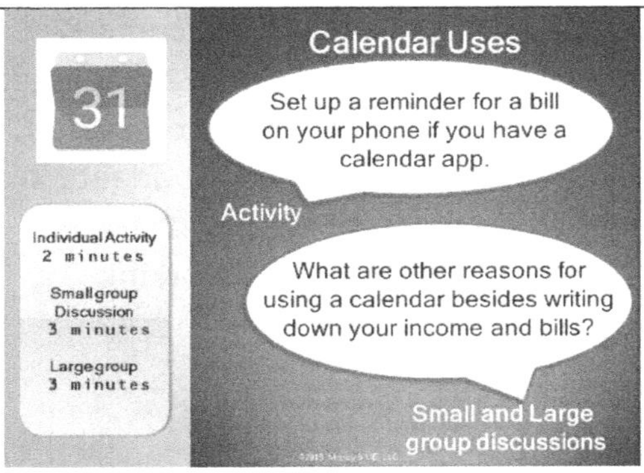

Participants will fill in their Income & Bills Calendars Template at home. Having their bills readily available will make it easier for them to complete this activity. Other uses for a calendar include writing down appointments, tracking habit changes, remembering birthdays, etc. Encourage them to schedule a follow-up for more help.

Slide 8

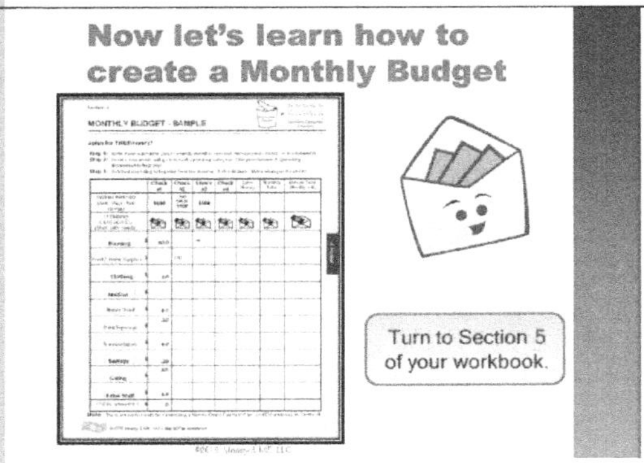

Monthly Budget

Have participants turn to Section 5 of their workbooks. During this part of the workshop they will learn more about the Monthly Budget and how to be a smart shopper. This may be the first-time participants have created written budgets. The Monthly Budget lays the FOUNDATION for the rest of the *Money & ME Program.*

Slide 9

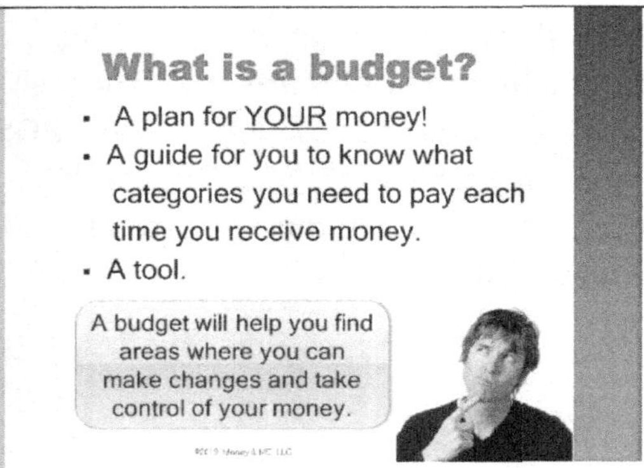

"Budget" might be a NEW or SCARY word for some participants. Remind them, a budget is a **"plan"** to help them with their money needs and goals. Making a budget does not happen immediately. Keys to their success are being patient with one another, working together, and adjusting their budgets as needed.

Slide 10

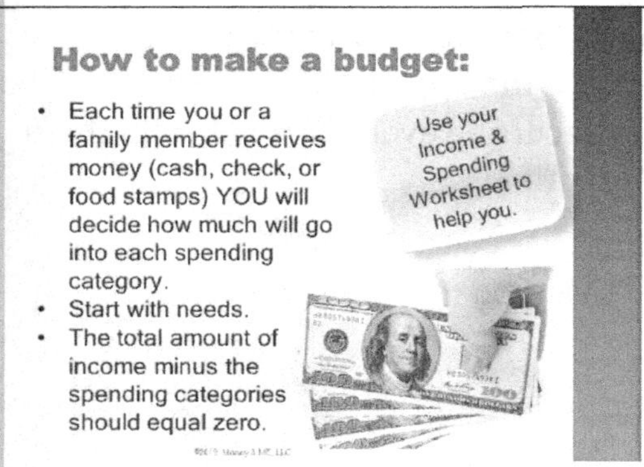

It is important for participants to realize they will NEED the amounts they write in their Income & Spending Worksheets for their budgets. They will need their Income & Bills Calendars to write down which week they get paid and which week their bills are due. These two worksheets will help them complete their Monthly Budgets.

Slide 11

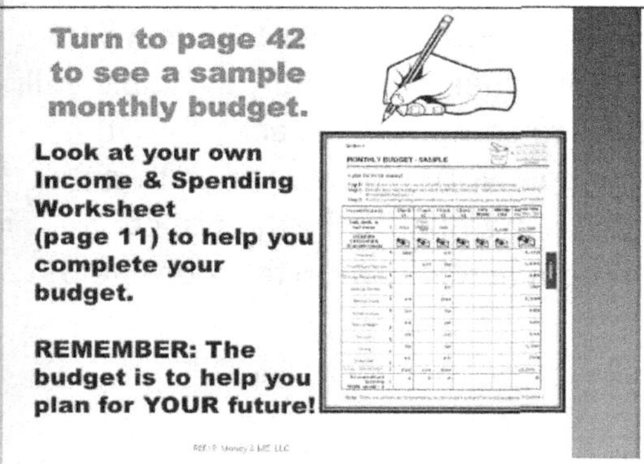

Budgets can be difficult. However, once the Income & Spending Worksheet as well as the Income & Bills Calendar are filled in, then the Monthly Budget can be completed. Let participants know they will begin building budgets, but they can make changes as they need. Making changes is normal. It will take a few months to have a working Monthly Budget.

Slide 12

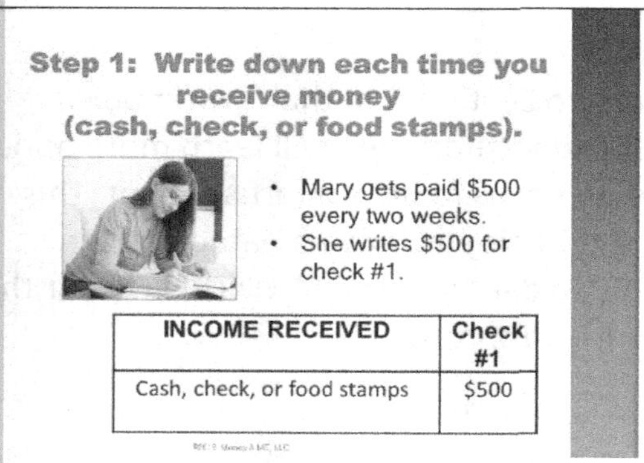

This worksheet is designed for multiple checks. It can be from one person having two jobs or from multiple people in the household. Each time a person receives a check, he or she needs to plan how it will be used.

Slide 13

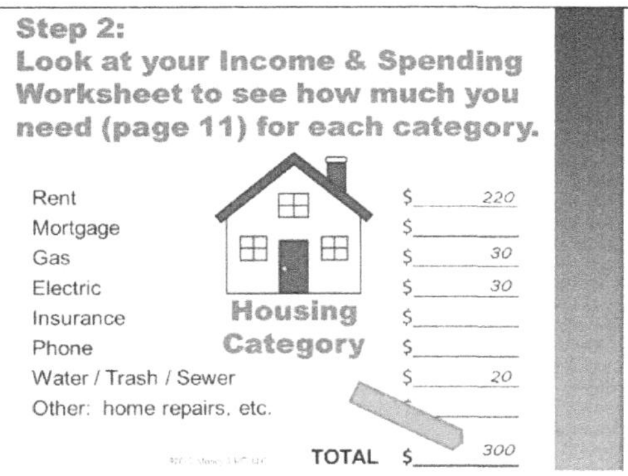

Acknowledge HOUSING can be a difficult area to make changes. However, if a person or family is spending more than 30% of its monthly income on housing it will greatly reduce other spending categories. Options to consider for reducing housing expenses may include moving to a different place, applying for subsidized housing, etc. Reason: Budget billing does not reduce overall expenses. Budget billing only spreads out payments. Home phones (landlines) should be listed in this category. Cell phones can be listed here or in the clothing and personal items section.

Slide 14

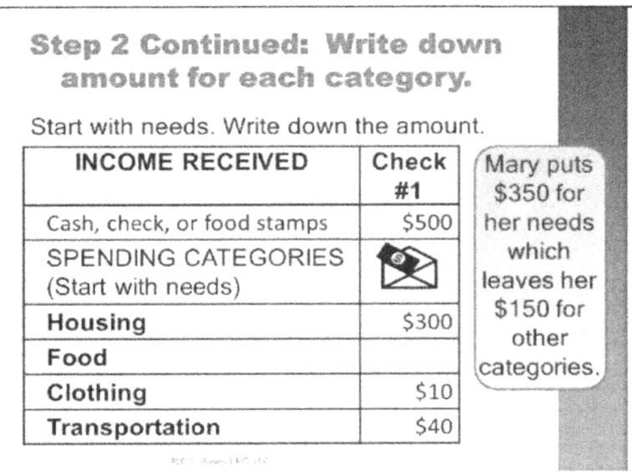

Make sure participants start with needs first!

Slide 15

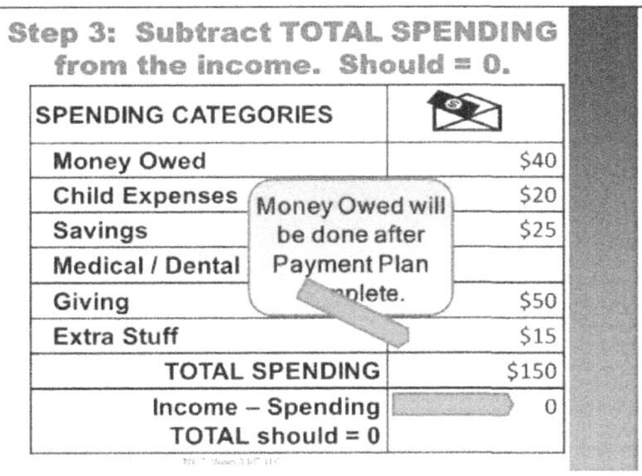

After the needs have been payed, the participants will need to make decisions on the other amounts. Have them use their Income & Spending Worksheet. NOTE: The Money Owed category cannot be completed until the Payment Plan is complete.

Slide 16

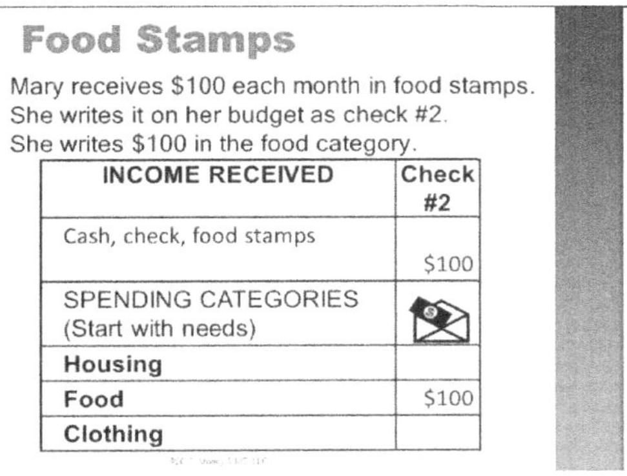

Food Stamps are considered income and will be designated for the food category.

Slide 17

Check #3

Mary gets $500.

INCOME RECEIVED	Check #3
Cash, check, or food stamps	$500
SPENDING CATEGORIES (Start with needs)	
Housing	
Food / Home Supplies	$20
Clothing / Personal Items	$75
Transportation	$20

She uses $115 for needs.

This leaves her $385 for the other categories.

With the third check (remember Food stamps was check #2), there are many ways this money could be designated. Encourage participants to do what works for them.

Slide 18

Continued from Check #3

SPENDING CATEGORIES	
Money Owed	$230
Child Expenses	$20
Medical / Dental	$15
Savings	$25
Giving	$50
Extra Stuff	$45
TOTAL SPENDING	$500
Income – Spending TOTAL should = 0	0

The amounts will go into your envelopes (if using cash).

The Payment Plan will be done in Section 5. Let participants know they will come back to complete their budgets.

Slide 19

Step 3: Subtract spending from income.

INCOME RECEIVED	Check #1	Check #2	Check #3
Cash, check, or food stamps	$500	$100	$500
SPENDING CATEGORIES (Start with needs)			
Housing	$300		
Food / Home Supplies		$100	$20
Clothing	$10		$75
Transportation	$40		$20
Money Owed	$40		$230
Child Expenses	$20		$20
Medical / Dental			$15
Savings	$25		$25
Giving	$50		$50
Extra Stuff	$15		$45
TOTAL SPENDING	$500	$100	$500
TOTAL should = 0	0	0	0

You will need to make changes to equal zero!

Let participants know they will probably need to make several changes until the income minus spending equals zero. Encourage them to use a pencil.

Slide 20

Another way to think about a budget

Think of the total amount of money you get each month like a bucket of water.

INCOME RECEIVED	Check #1	Check #2	Check #3
Cash, check, or food stamps	$500	$100	$500

Food stamps is income.

Step 1 is writing down their monthly incomes. We relate monthly income to a bucket of water that they fill each month. They only get a certain "amount" of water to make their budgets.

Slide 21

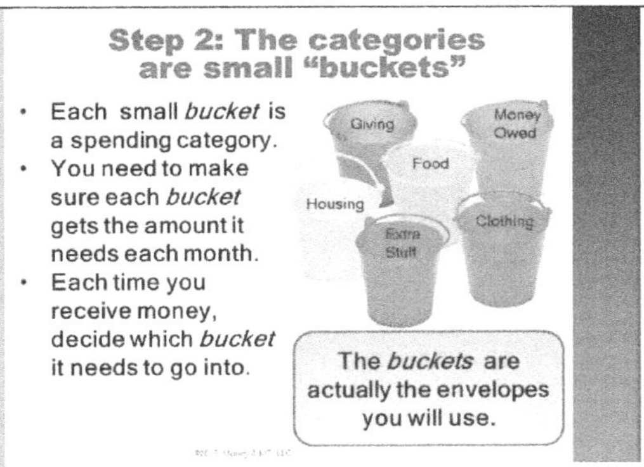

Step 2 - Dividing up a total amount of income into different spending categories can be confusing.
Using smaller buckets can help participants think about how much money they should put into each bucket. This will help them develop their budgets. Small buckets represent the envelopes in the Cash Envelope System.

Slide 22

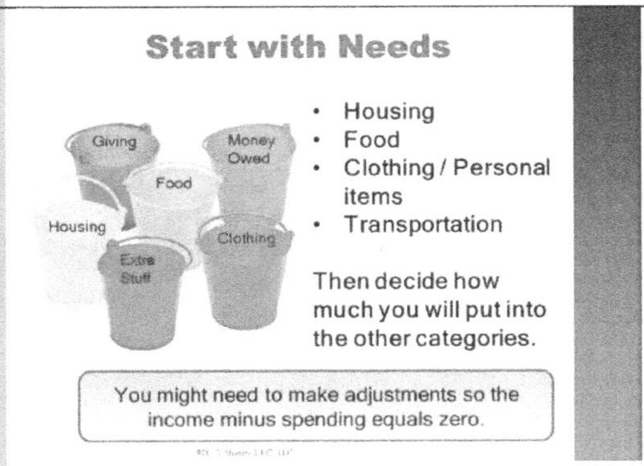

It is important for participants to pay their "fixed" amounts first. Fixed amounts can be changed, but it will require effort and take some time. Other amounts that are NOT fixed may be easily changed.

Slide 23

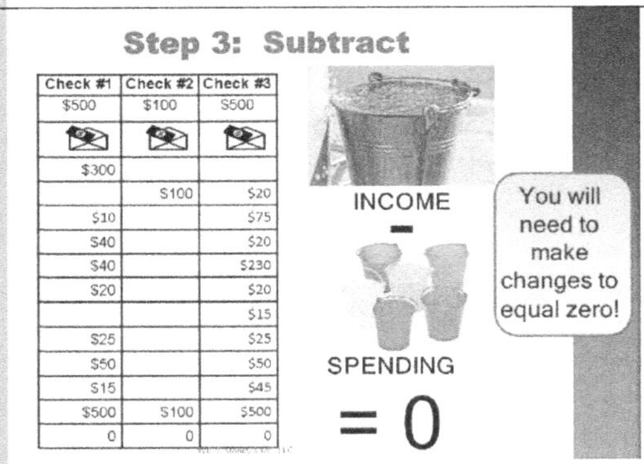

Step 3 – Participants need to subtract their spending from their income to make sure their income matches their spending. It is very common for people to overspend. They need to make adjustments to their budgets and learn how to live within the budgets they create.

Slide 24

Encourage participants to live within the budgets they create. If they spend money that is not in their budgets it is like a leaky bucket and they won't have enough money at the end of the month. A leaky bucket can also happen when they spend money on their wants instead of their needs.

Slide 25

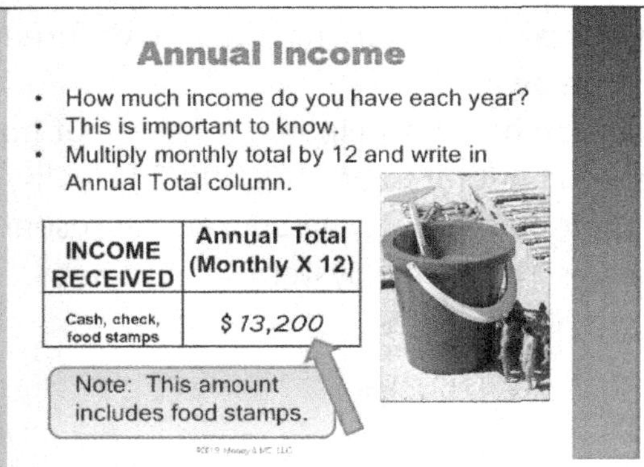

It is important for participants to start figuring out their annual incomes.

Slide 26

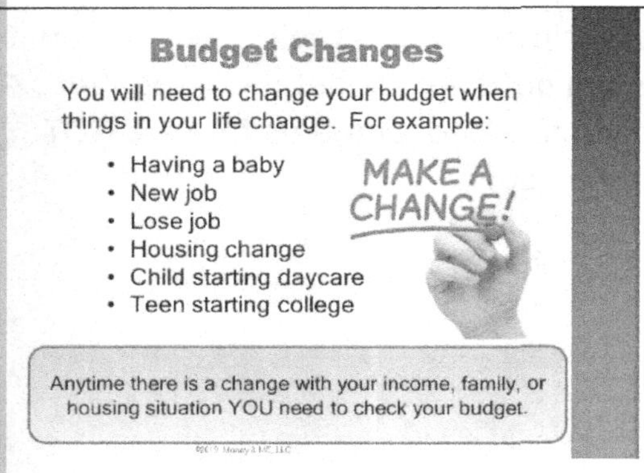

People need to make changes to their budgets when their income or spending changes. It is important to realize that this is not something you do one time in your life and you are done. It is an ongoing process of change as life changes.

Slide 27

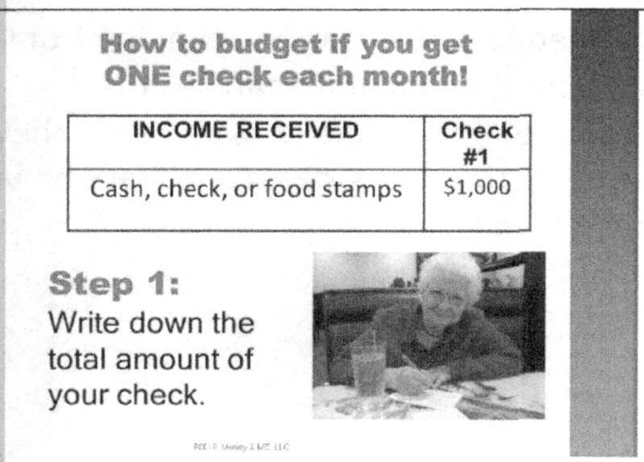

This is an example for how a person should budget if he/she gets one check. It would seem simple, but many participants had questions, so it was added for clarification.

Slide 28

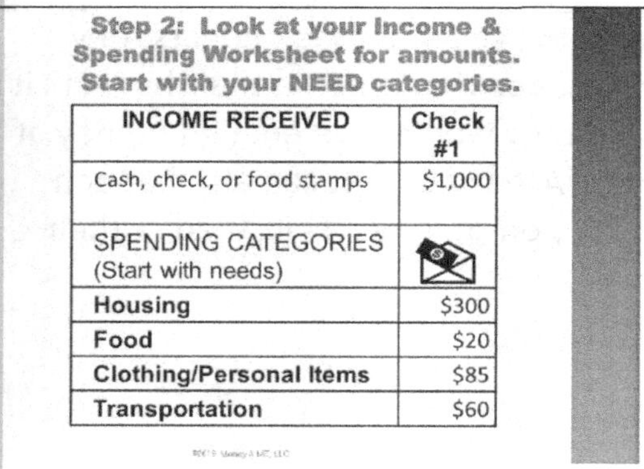

Encourage participants to start with their needs to make sure those categories get paid first!

Slide 29

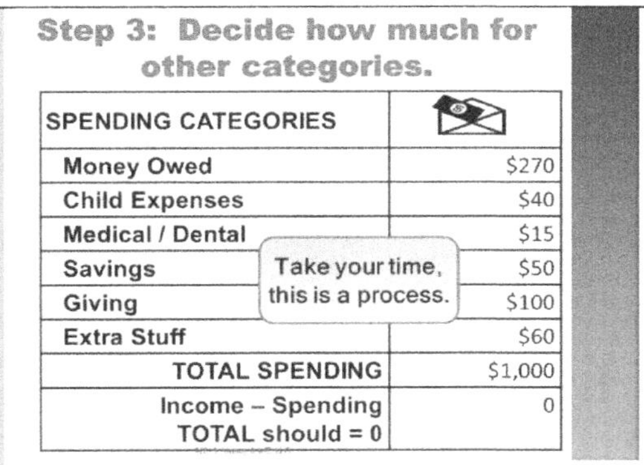

The participants can then adjust the other amounts until the income minus spending equals zero.

Slide 30

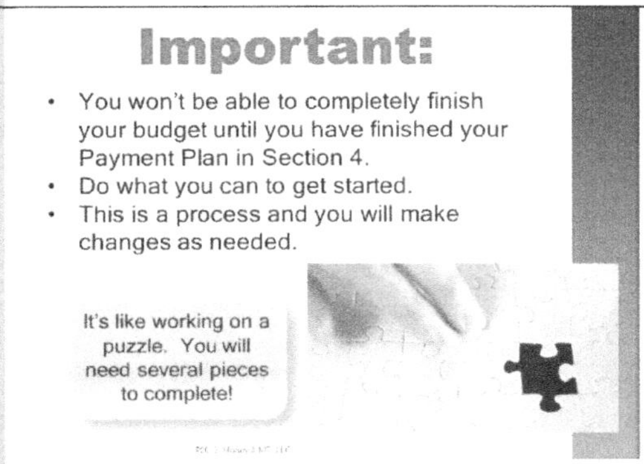

It is important for participants to know that they need to complete their Payment Plan amounts before they can finalize their budgets.

Slide 31

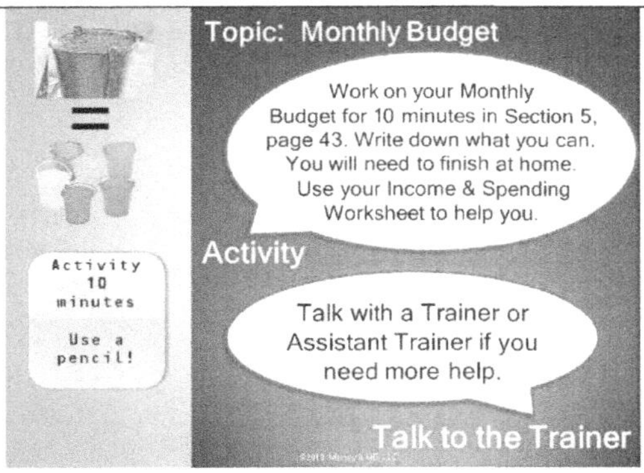

Once again, DO NOT skip the discussion activities. This is where REAL learning takes place. Encourage participants to share what they have learned. Participants will not have enough time to FINISH their budgets. This is a time to get them started. This may be a hard concept for some people. If you are able to have people come back and meet with a Coach, let them know how they can get additional help. Allow 10 minutes for this activity and discussion.

Slide 32

Cash Envelope System

The next section will introduce the Cash Envelope System.

Slide 33

Emphasize to participants the importance of doing the Monthly Budget because the Cash Envelope System is built around a completed budget.

Slide 34

The budget will tell them how much money will go into each envelope after they have labeled their envelopes.

Slide 35

This slide illustrates how paper money goes in and out of the envelopes when spending.

Slide 36

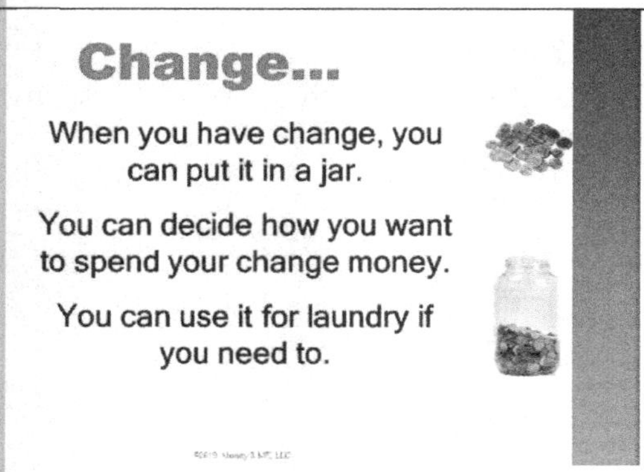

Coins can tear apart the envelopes over time. The participants can put the coins into jars and save that money for something else.

Slide 37

It is SO important that participants learn to say NO when they are out of money. Practice with them several times. Make it fun…like a game!

Slide 38

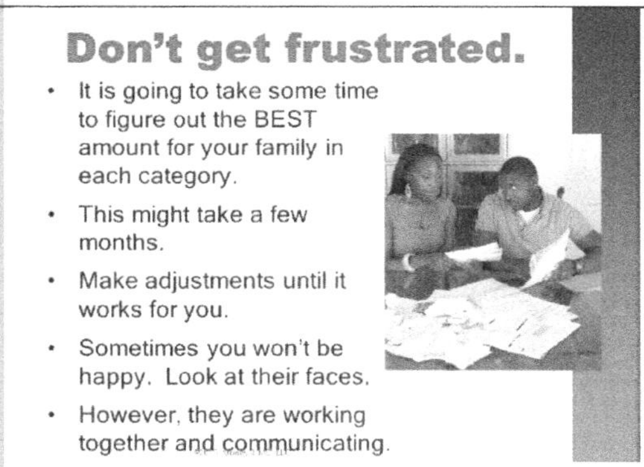

Encourage them not to quit. Remember the bicycle – if you fall, get up and start again.

Slide 39

If the participants need more envelopes to help them save for special things, they can purchase extras. Let them know it is important to keep this system simple or it won't work. The more complicated they make it, the less likely they are to use it.

Slide 40

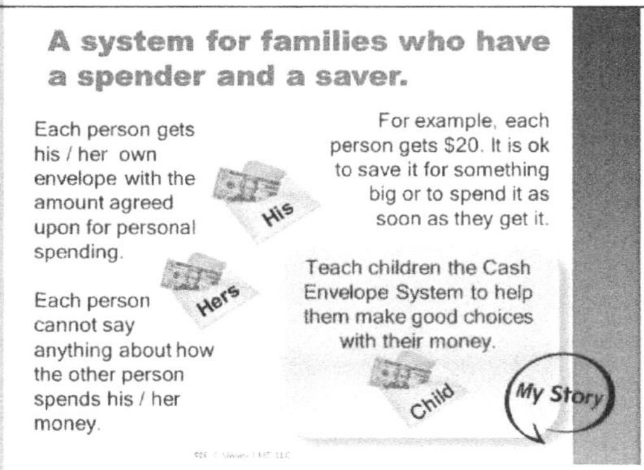

This is a great system for families who have a spender and a saver. They can also start teaching their children about the Cash Envelope System to help children make good choices. **Trainer Story: Share a brief story about whether you are a spender or a saver. What lessons have you learned?**

Slide 41

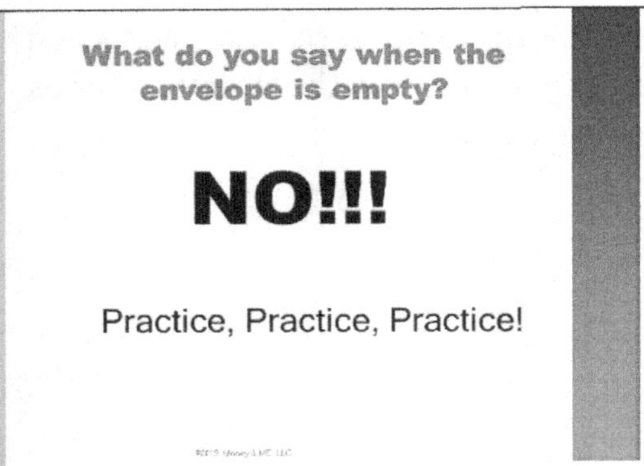

Keep them practicing. It seems silly, but this is a great learning technique.

Slide 42

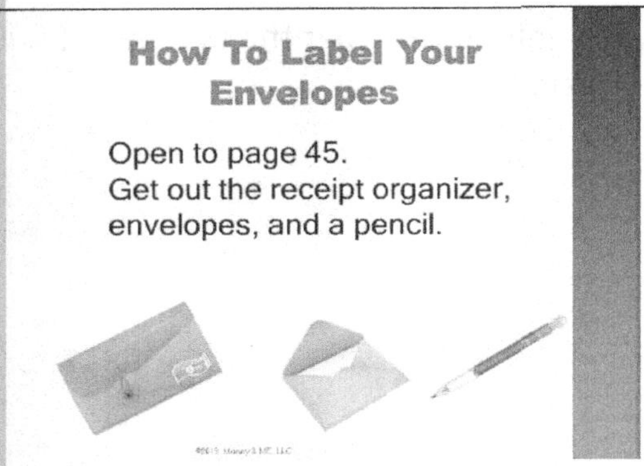

You are getting the participants ready for the next activity.

Slide 43

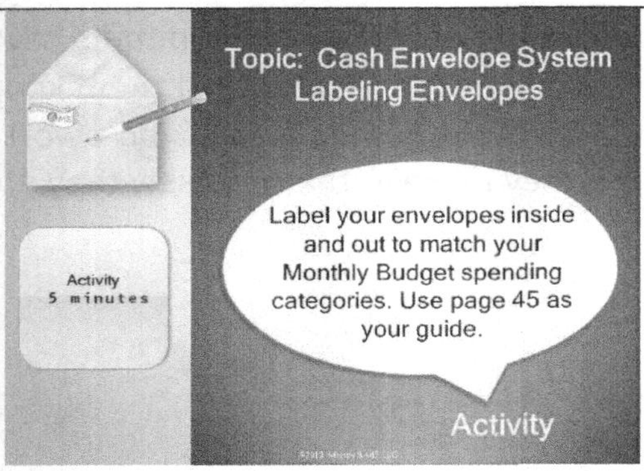

Trainer and Assistant Trainer need to keep track of the time. Adjust so you stay on target.

Slide 44

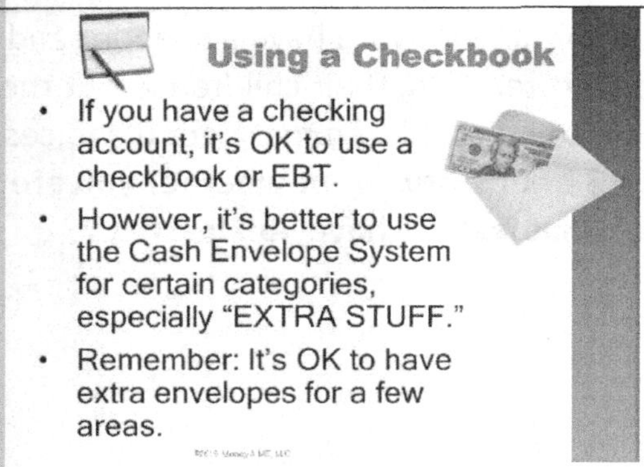

Most of the participants will not have a checkbook, but if they do, we want them to know it is OK to use it. The quicker they pay their bills, the less likely they are to have their money lost or stolen.

Slide 45

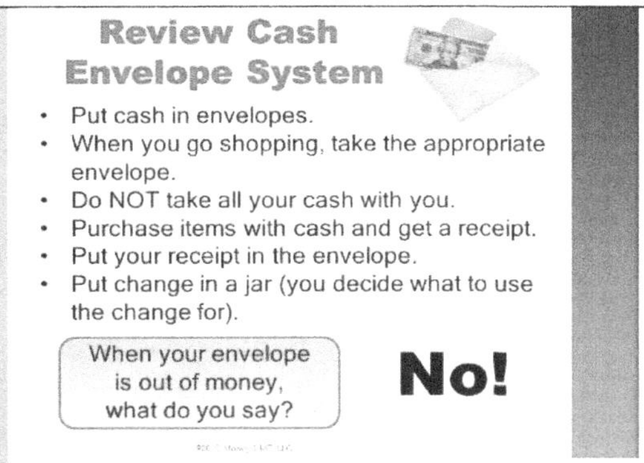

People remember through repetition. It is good to review. Get the class really involved in saying no. Keep asking them...What do you say when you're out of money? NO.

Slide 46

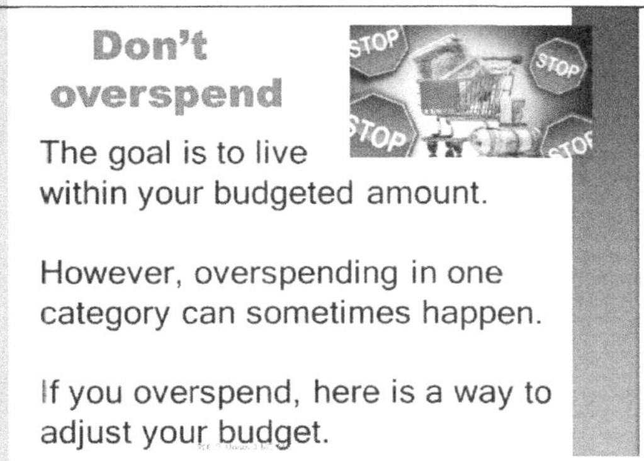

It is important for participants to work toward living within their new budgets. Trainers should strongly encourage this new habit.

Slide 47

This is an example of how they can make changes and adjustments if needed. However, encourage them to live within their budgets.

Slide 48

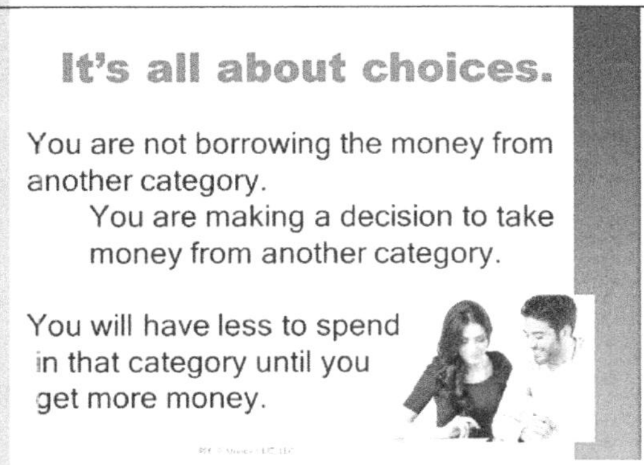

We want them to understand they have choices and are in control of their budgets. It is not to control them. They can make adjustments as needed.

Slide 49

SPENDING RECORD BY CATEGORY

- Turn to Section 5, page 46 to see the sample.
- This is VERY important if you are using a checkbook or EBT Card.
- It will help you NOT overspend.
- There are 10 worksheets.
- One for each spending category.

Look at your Income & Spending Worksheet to help you.

Spending Record By Category

They can use regular notebook paper if they wish.

Slide 50

Part One

Spending Category	Monthly Amount Needed	Amount from Check #1	Amount from Check #2	Amount from Check #3	Amount from Check #4	Extra
Housing	$300	$300				

You will use one worksheet for each category. There are 10 worksheets in your workbook.

Write down the category in the first column.

Write down the amount you will need each month in the second column.
Write how much you will put into this category from each check.

Participants need to use their Monthly Budgets to write the correct amounts in the "Monthly Spending By Category." It is ALWAYS important for them to see how much they are spending a year in each category.

Slide 51

Part Two

Date	Person or Place Money Spent	Money Out	Money In	Amount Left
12/1	Money In		$300	$300
12/2	Water	$20		$280
12/5	Rent	$220		$60
12/9	Gas / Electric	$60		0

Step 1: Each time you get paid, write down the date and the amount in the "Money In" column. This s is a "+."
Step 2: Use your Income & Spending Worksheet to see all the items related to each category.
Step 3: Each time you spend money write the date, person or place money spent, and the amount in the "Money Out" column.
Step 4: Subtract each time you spend money so you know how much you have in the category.

The idea is for participants to start tracking the income and spending for each individual category.

Slide 52

Part Three

Repeat this when you get more money, and when you pay for things.

No!

Date	Type of Expense	Money Out	Money In	Amount Left
12/1	Money In		$300	$300
12/2	Water	$20		$280
12/5	Rent	$220		$60
12/9	Gas / Electric	$60		0
1/1	Money In		$300	$300
12/22	Rent	$220		$80

- The balance number should equal what is in your envelope *(not counting whatever was put into a jar).*
- When you are out of money, what do you say?

The participants need to add and subtract how much money they are putting in their envelopes and how much they are spending. Balance should match the amount of money they have left in their envelopes (not counting whatever change was put into a jar). Using the note pad, an app, and sales receipts will help them with this task.

Slide 53

Spending Record by Category Worksheets will be done at home.

- It will take some time to complete these worksheets.
- You can use regular notebook paper after the first month.
- You can also use an app to help you.

The participants will need more information and time to complete this activity. Encourage them to do it at home.

Slide 54

Slide 55

Copyright Information

© 2019 Money & ME, LLC
This document and content to which this copyright notice is attached is protected by United States and worldwide copyright laws and treaty provisions.
No part of this program may be copied, reproduced, modified, adapted, published, or transmitted in any form without prior written permission.

E-mail
Contactus@MoneyandME.cash

Do NOT change the content of this program! Each component was designed specifically for low-income people, tested, and proven to guide them to make changes and take control of their money. By changing the content you are cheating someone from receiving the full benefit. We welcome your feedback. You may e-mail Contactus@MoneyandME.cash.

Session 6: Take Control

Slide 1

Slide 2

Take Control

This is a fun slide. If the trainer is comfortable doing this pose, it is fun for the participants to see. Encourage them to do the same.

Slide 3

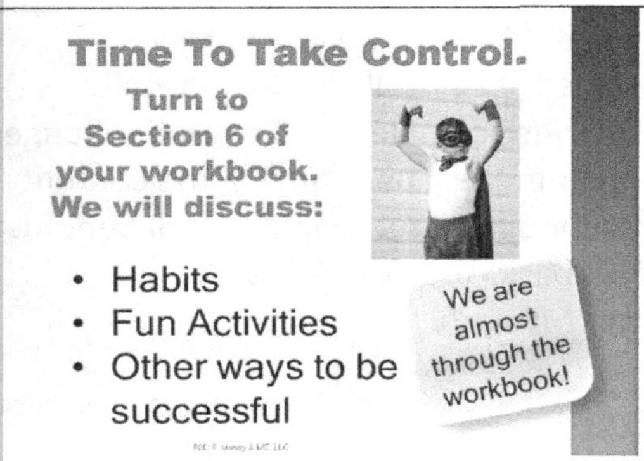

There are three topics in this last section. Let participants know they are doing good, and they are almost through the workbook.

Slide 4

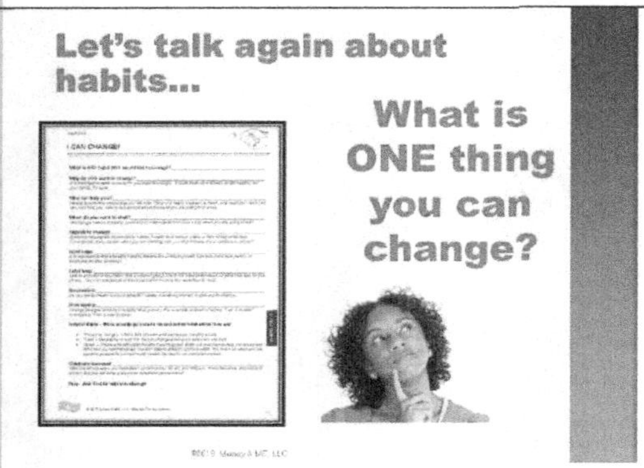

Change a Habit.

Money & ME is designed to change lives. Changing ONE habit can change a life, a family, and a generation. However, this can be a very emotional and sensitive issue. Do not get into arguments with people. Just encourage them to look at themselves and decide one thing they can change.

Slide 5

Changing a habit IS extremely difficult to do. It will feel strange and it is important to acknowledge that it will feel funny. The following slides will lead into an activity where they will fill out an "I Can Change!" worksheet.

Slide 6

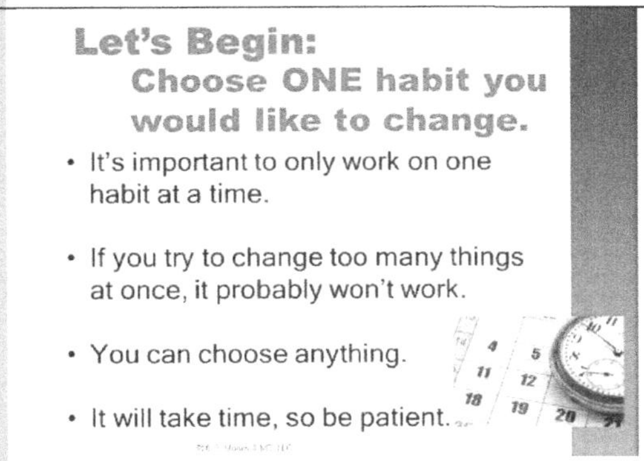

Have participants choose ONE thing they would like to work on. After they have been successful for 90 days, they can choose another habit to change. If they try to change too much at once, they most likely will fail.

Slide 7

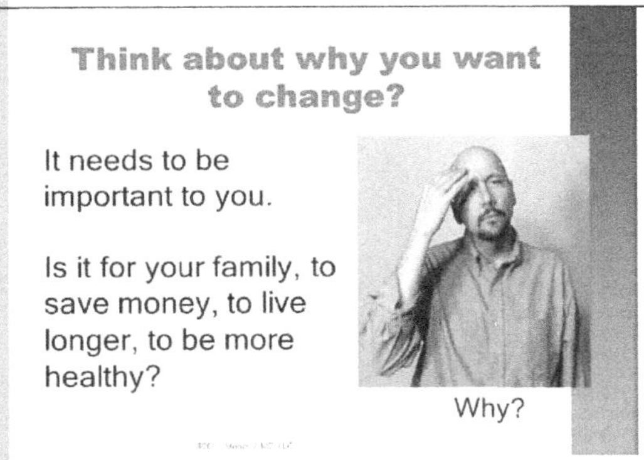

It is important for participants to think about "THE WHY." Without acknowledging WHY they want to change, they won't stick to their new habits. This picture is the sign for "why" in American Sign Language (ASL).

Slide 8

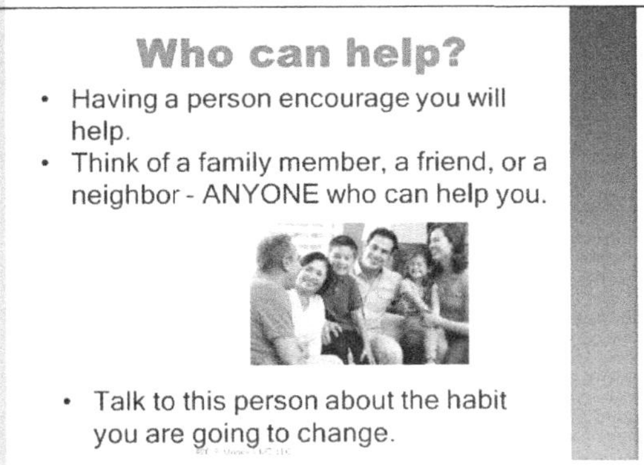

EVERYONE needs someone to encourage him / her. Have participants think who is in their lives who can encourage and still hold them accountable. They will write this person's name during the next activity.

Slide 9

Many times, there are people in our lives who are bad influences. Just being around them leads to bad behaviors. Have participants think who they need to stay away from.

Slide 10

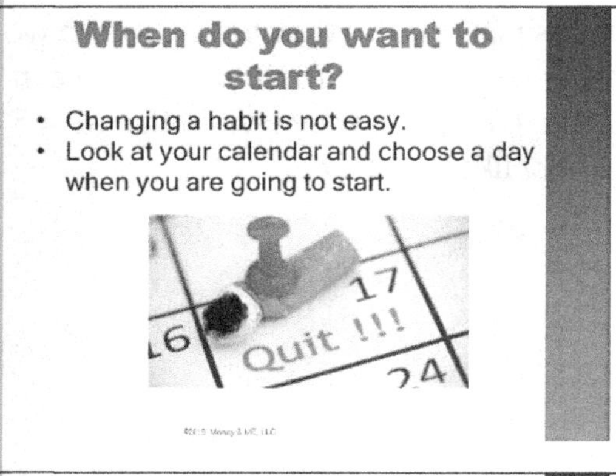

It is important to identify when they would like to start this change. Have them think about their schedules, holidays, and other things happening in their lives. Only they can truly decide the best day to start.

Slide 11

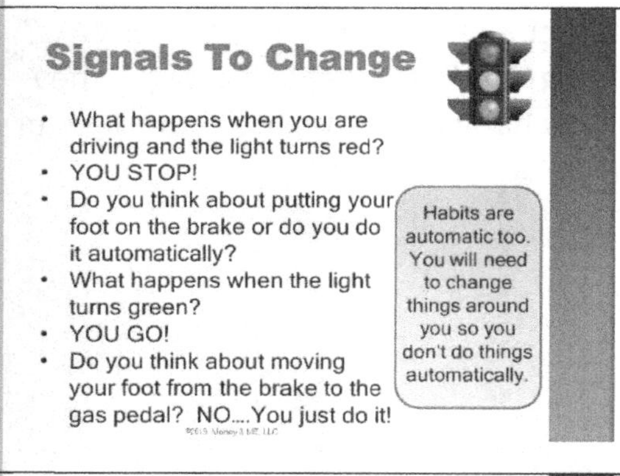

We do some things automatically. To stop doing things automatically you will have to change things around.

Slide 12

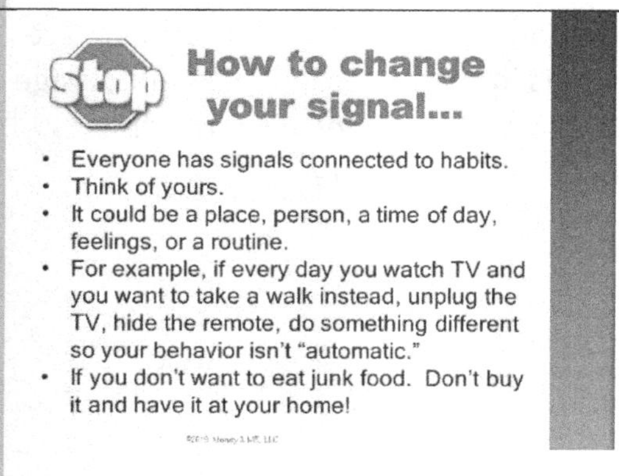

All of us have signals, also known as "cues" or "triggers," that connect us to our habits. Have participants think about various triggers in their own lives.

Slide 13

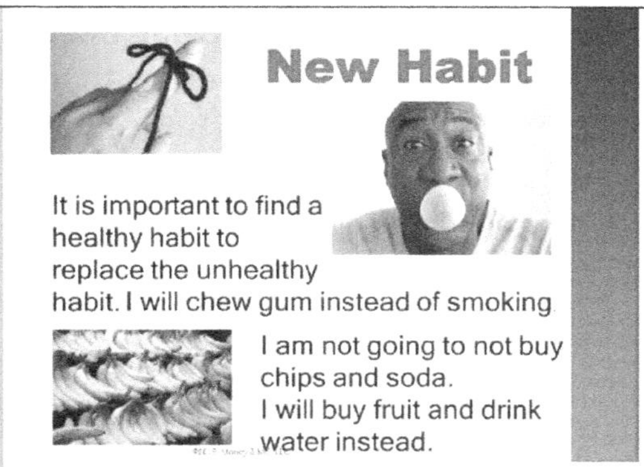

It is important to replace an unhealthy habit with a healthy habit. Let them think of something that would be good for them.

Slide 14

Encourage participants to talk to their doctors about ideas on stopping smoking or losing weight. They might get a prescription for something that would help them overcome the physical addiction they have with a habit. They could check the internet (at the library) for support groups or other ways to help them. There are places to get nicotine patches for free as well as other aids to assist with bad habits. There are several "non-smoking" apps that will illustrate how much money they have saved and how much their health has improved.

Slide 15

Many people are inspired by being creative. Encourage them to make up a song, jingle or create some artwork as a visual or auditory reminder about their new habit.

Slide 16

Create a visual reminder on your phone can help you remember the new behavior you are working on.

Slide 17

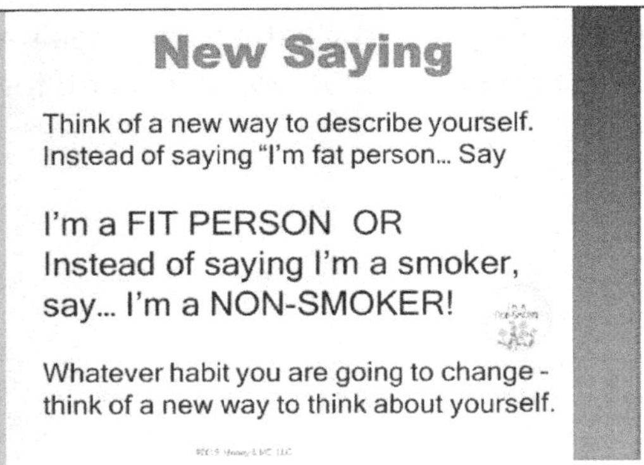

If people think of themselves as smokers, or being fat, or lazy, they can become what they think. Encourage them to create a new saying about themselves: I'm a non-smoker, I am getting in shape, I am active, etc.

Slide 18

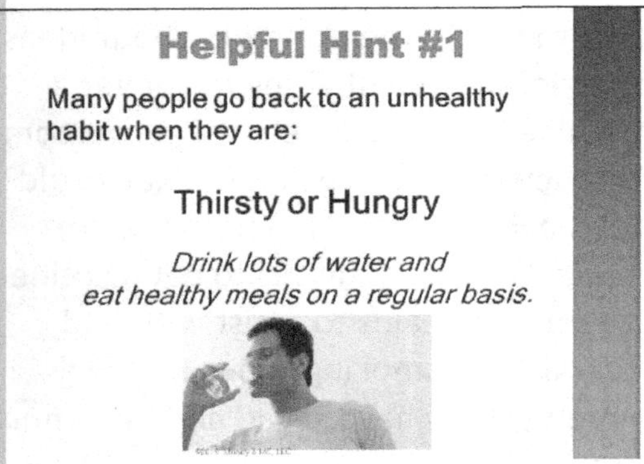

It is so hard to stick to a new habit when you are thirsty or hungry. Encourage participants to drink plenty of water and eat healthy meals regularly.

Slide 19

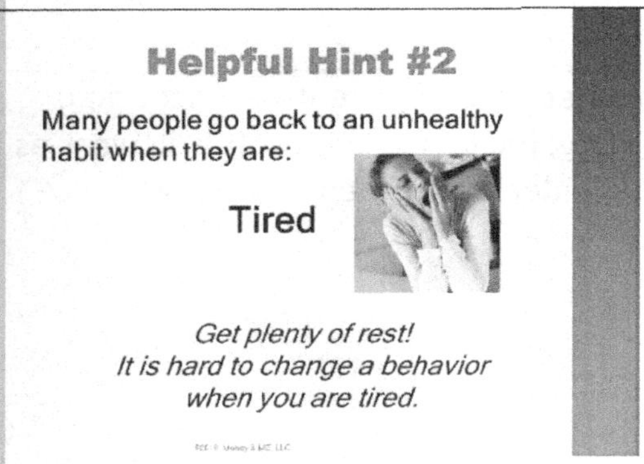

Another obstacle in changing an old habit is tiredness. Encourage them to get plenty of rest.

Slide 20

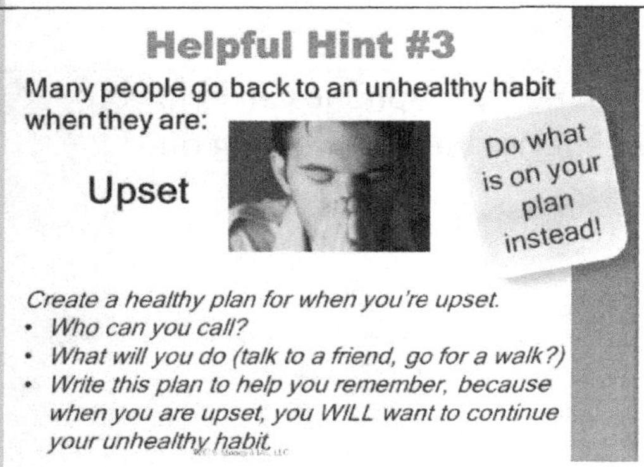

When a person gets upset for any reason, the impulse may be to resume a bad habit. Encourage them to develop a plan when they are upset so they don't go back to their old habits.

Slide 21	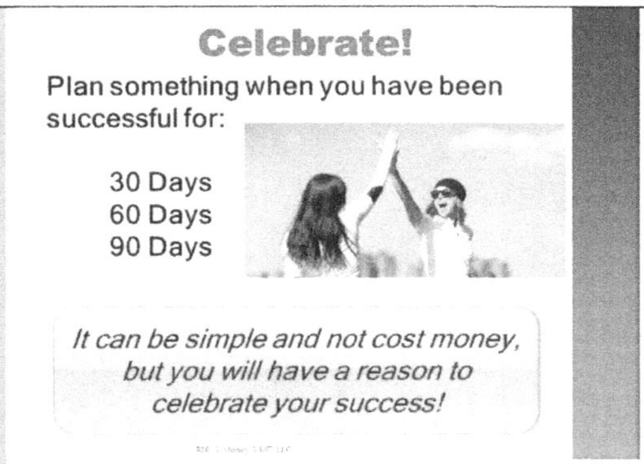	Having something to look forward to when the habit has been successfully changed is EXTREMLY IMPORTANT. It can be buying new clothes for losing weight, doing a special activity, getting a small treat for yourself. Let them figure out what success would be for them!
Slide 22	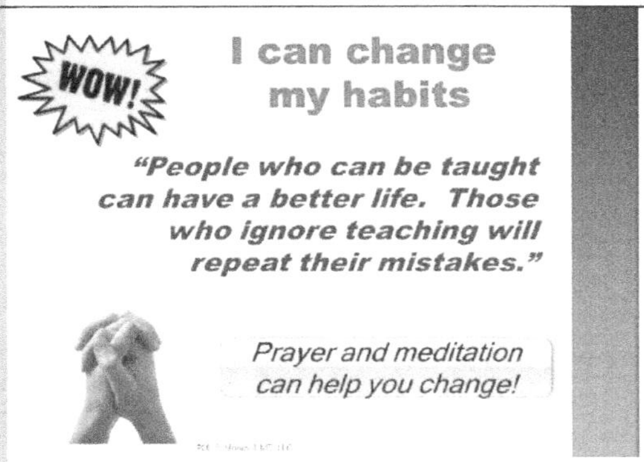	Let participants know that prayer and meditation can help them change.
Slide 23	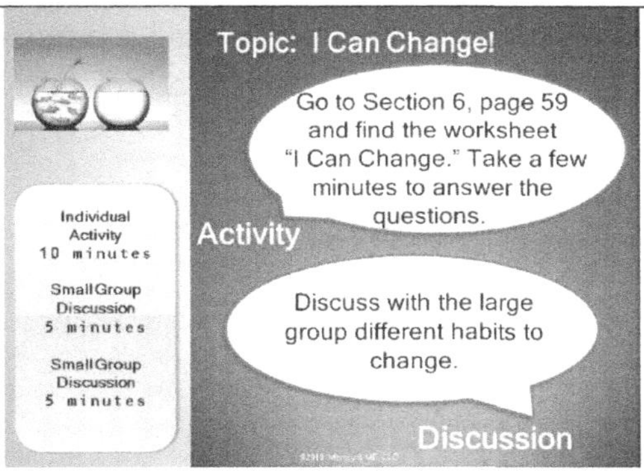	Once again, DO NOT skip the discussion activities. This is where REAL learning takes place. Encourage participants to share what they have learned.
Slide 24	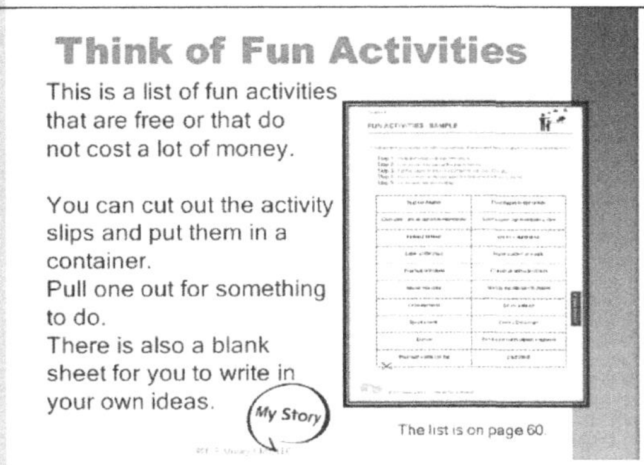	**Free or Low-Cost Activities** **Trainer Story: Share an activity that you like to do for free or that costs very little money.**

Slide 25

Libraries are amazing resources that might be overlooked. Let participants know libraries are free and offer lots of things to do.

Slide 26

A lot of times people say they have to stay at home because they don't have money. Instead, encourage them to think of activities they could do for free in their own communities.

Slide 27

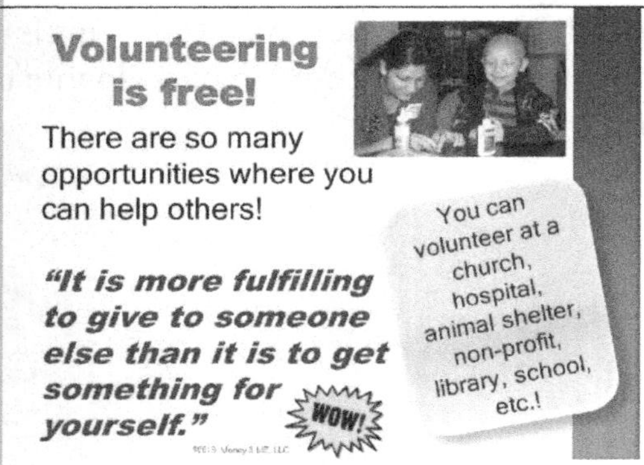

There are LOTS of opportunities to volunteer to help people stay active, give back to their communities, and improve their own self-worth.

Slide 28

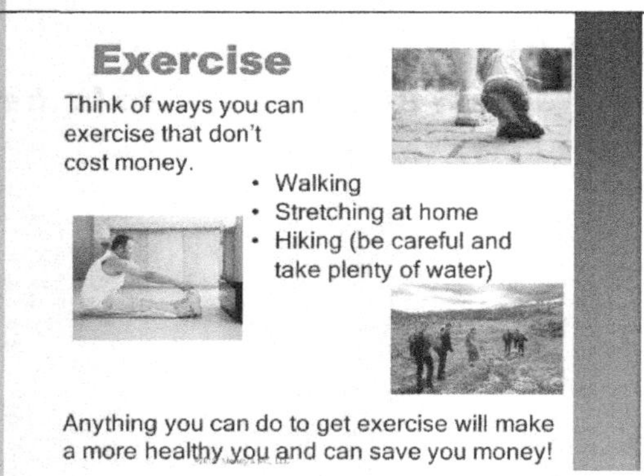

Exercise is VERY important and doesn't have to cost money. Remember we are teaching them areas where they can make changes.

Slide 29	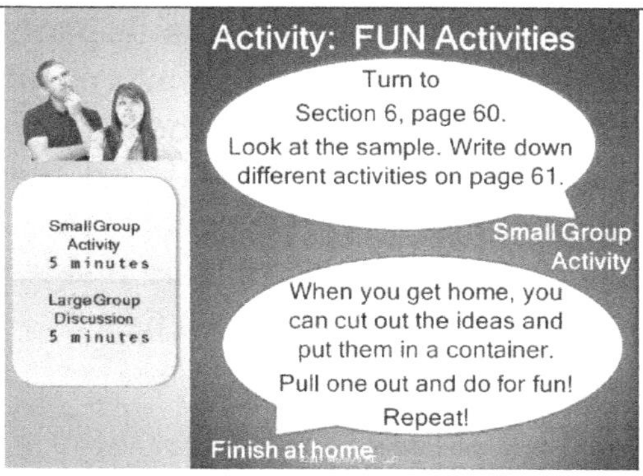	Many times low-income people sit at home and do nothing (or watch TV) because they don't know about free activities. This allows them to think about things they can do that do not cost a lot of money. If your class is running out of time, let them do this activity at home for homework.
Slide 30	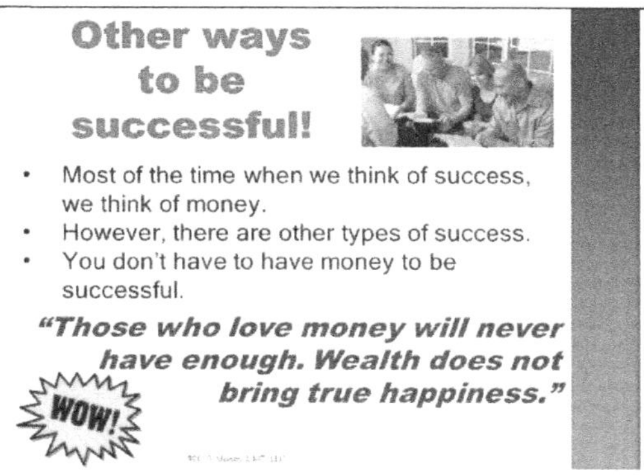	**Other ways to be successful**. Many participants will never be financially wealthy. We want them to understand they can be successful in other ways. The next three slides discuss different types of success.
Slide 31	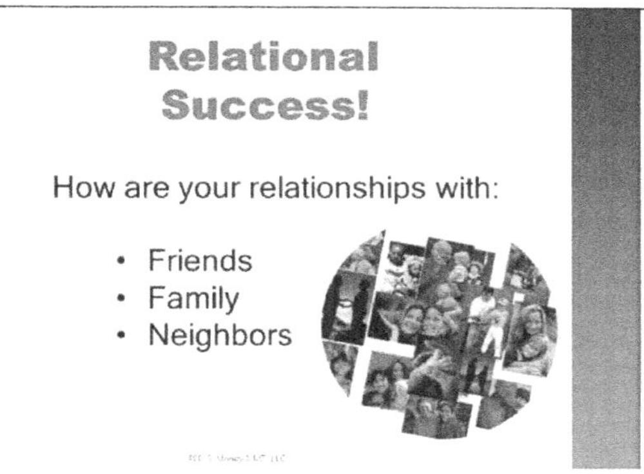	Just read through this slide. Do not spend a lot of time here.
Slide 32	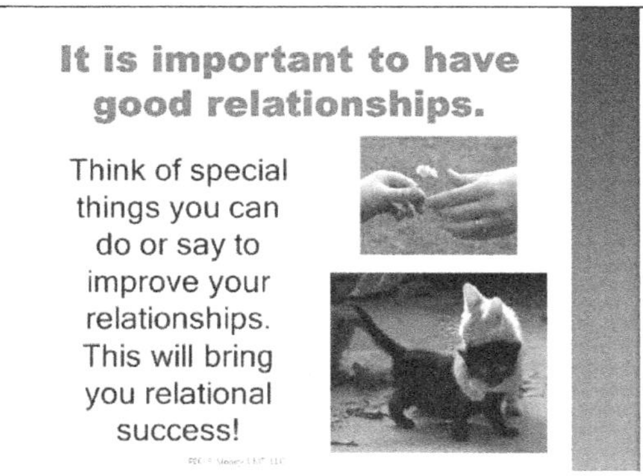	God wants us to be in good relationships with one another. It is important to build one another up.

Slide 33

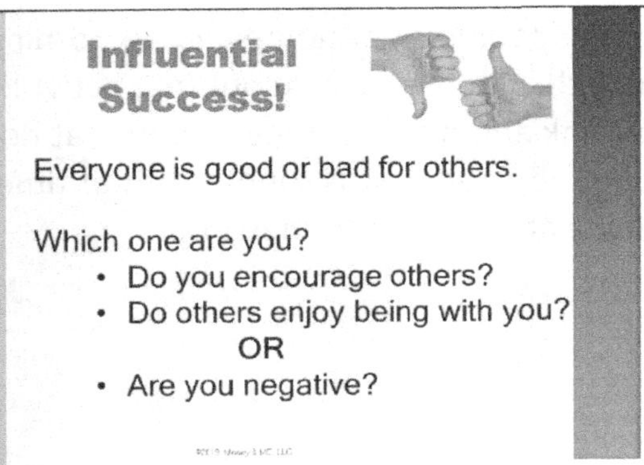

The word "influential" may be hard for some participants to understand. The visual of a thumbs up or a thumbs down is to get them thinking about people who are good for them and others who are not. The reverse is also true. Ask them if they are good or bad for those around them. Are they affecting people in a good or bad way? What are things they could change? This is leading them to the next discussion time.

Slide 34

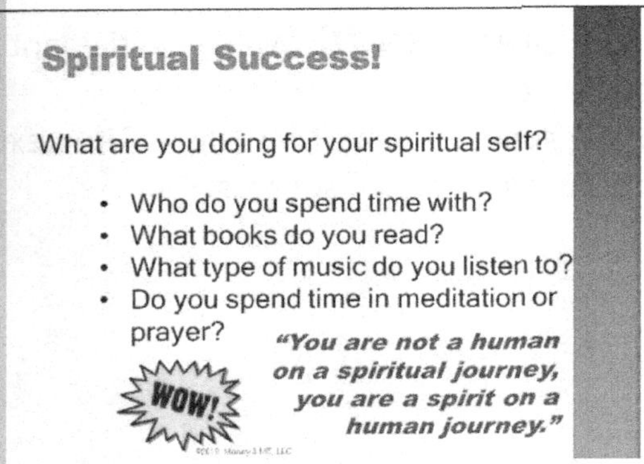

As a trainer, you want them to not only handle their money better but improve their spiritual life as well. Talk about different ways to improve their spiritual life.

Slide 35

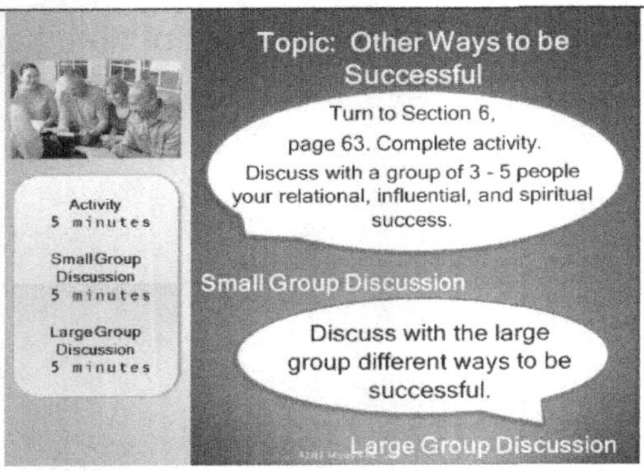

This is the last discussion of the class and is designed to help participants identify areas in their lives where they are wealthy. They may never have a LOT of money, but they should be encouraged to think of themselves as wealthy in other ways. Encourage them to discuss in their small groups and then share with others.

Slide 36

Encourages others to be whatever it is God desires for them.

Slide 37

Have people like page on facebook!

Slide 38

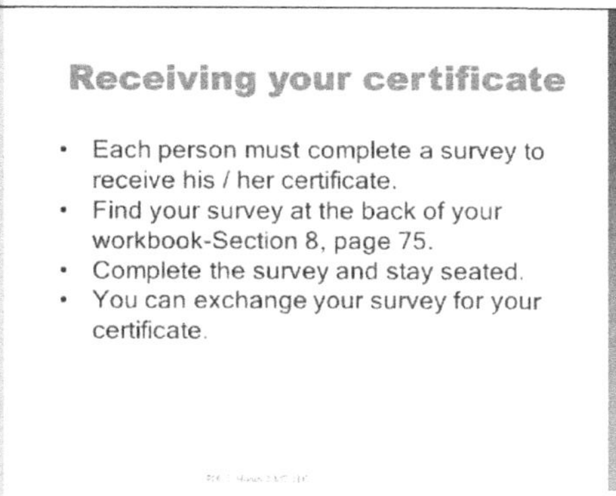

It can get very chaotic toward the end. Have the participants complete their surveys and stay seated until the Assistant Trainer calls their names. They can pick up their participation gifts / incentives.

Slide 39

Certificates

Certificates are so important. Many of our participants have not completed programs such as high school, higher education, etc. The participant will appreciate the participation gift / incentive. This is something lasting for them. Some participants have been mandated by a probation officer, case manager, or court to complete a program. This certificate can also be used for proof of completion.

Slide 40

Promoting the Program.

A picture is worth a thousand words and it benefits everyone to promote the program. Sponsors, organizations, and individuals all like to see people learning to get in control of their money and their lives. If someone is not comfortable having his or her photo taken, do NOT force the issue. Maybe he or she could be the photographer. E-mail photo and a few sentences about your program to info@MoneyandME.cash and also post on Facebook. Thank you!

Slide 41

Slide 42

Do NOT change the content of this program! Each component was designed specifically for low-income people, tested, and proven to guide them to make changes and take control of their money. By changing the content you are cheating someone from receiving the full benefit. We welcome your feedback. You may e-mail Info@MoneyandME.cash.

Made in United States
North Haven, CT
05 November 2026

21763969R00046